57 HOURS

57 HOURS

a survivor's account of
the Moscow hostage drama

VESSELIN NEDKOV and PAUL WILSON

VIKING
CANADA

VIKING CANADA

Penguin Group (Canada), a division of Pearson Penguin Canada Inc.,
10 Alcorn Avenue, Toronto, Ontario M4V 3B2

Penguin Group (U.K.), 80 Strand, London WC2R 0RL, England
Penguin Group (U.S.), 375 Hudson Street, New York, New York 10014, U.S.A.
Penguin Group (Australia) Inc., 250 Camberwell Road, Camberwell, Victoria 3124, Australia
Penguin Group (Ireland), 25 St. Stephen's Green, Dublin 2, Ireland
Penguin Books India (P) Ltd, 11, Community Centre, Panchsheel Park,
New Delhi – 110 017, India
Penguin Group (New Zealand), cnr Rosedale and Airborne Roads, Albany, Auckland 1310,
New Zealand
Penguin Books (South Africa) (Pty) Ltd, 24 Sturdee Avenue, Rosebank 2196, South Africa

Penguin Group, Registered Offices: 80 Strand, London WC2R 0RL, England

First published 2003

1 2 3 4 5 6 7 8 9 10 (FR)

Copyright © Vesselin Nedkov and Paul Wilson, 2003

Manufactured in Canada.

NATIONAL LIBRARY OF CANADA CATALOGUING IN PUBLICATION

Nedkov, Vesselin, 1974–
57 hours : a survivor's account of the Moscow hostage drama / Vesselin Nedkov and Paul Wilson.

Includes bibliographical references and index.
ISBN 0-670-04435-0

1. Nedkov, Vesselin, 1974– 2. Hostages—Russia (Federation)—Moscow—Biography.
3. Chechnya (Russia)—History—Civil war, 1994–
I. Wilson, Paul, 1941– II. Title. III. Title: Fifty-seven hours.

DK601.2.N42 2003   947'.31086   C2003-905116-1

Visit the Penguin Group (Canada) website at **www.penguin.ca**

To the memory of the innocent victims
of the Moscow hostage-taking

CONTENTS

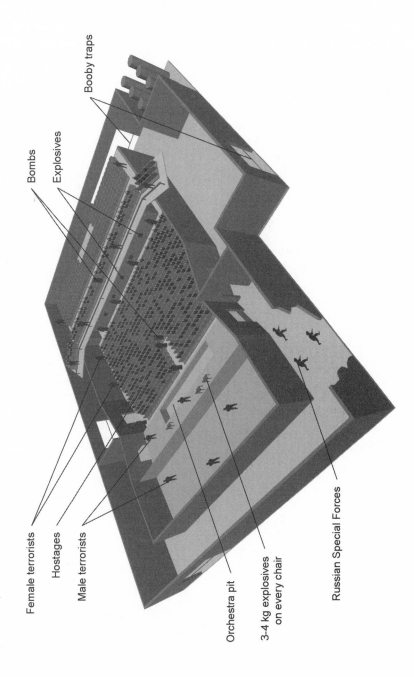

Female terrorists

Hostages

Male terrorists

Bombs

Explosives

Booby traps

Orchestra pit

3-4 kg explosives
on every chair

Russian Special Forces

FLOORPLAN OF THE HOUSE OF CULTURE

INTRODUCTION

When we first started working on this book, I was apprehensive. It was only a couple of months after the horrific events in a Moscow theatre when, along with eight hundred other people, I was taken hostage and held for two and a half days by a band of Chechen terrorists who threatened to kill us all if the Russian government didn't withdraw its troops from Chechnya. I survived, but there were many who didn't.

Whenever I thought about those traumatic days, I found myself becoming agitated and upset. At first I thought it might be enough to try to shut it out of my mind. Yet regardless of how hard I tried, I found I couldn't escape—certain images and sounds kept recurring in my brain. Sometimes a memory would be triggered by an incident, or a place. I would be on the Toronto subway, for instance, or in a busy street or a crowded room, and suddenly I would break out in a sweat, my heart pounding, and I would begin scanning the crowd for signs of danger, or searching for the nearest exit, the quickest way out, just in case.

Now, almost a year later, such moments are rare, but they still occur. Why, then, did I decide to work on this book, knowing that it would force me to relive the experience again and again, not just whenever a memory happened to resurface, but deliberately, almost every day? The decision came gradually, as I came to understand, intuitively at first, and later rationally, that suppressing my memories was not the answer. Unless I embraced the experience and tried to make sense of it, I knew that it would continue to haunt me in unpredictable and ultimately harmful ways.

But there was another reason for writing this book. It may sound like a cliché, but I have come to realize that part of the purpose behind terrorist acts like the one I lived through is to put whole societies on edge, to keep everyone looking over their shoulders, to force us all to live with a level of fear that can erupt, at any moment, into irrational terror. I came to understand that if I, and others, succumbed to this state of mind, the terrorists would have achieved an important part of their purpose. By sharing my experience with others, I hope to make a small contribution to defeating, or at least deflecting, their aims.

Terrorism can hold us all hostage, whether we are directly involved in an incident or not. I have learned that this current war on terror, whatever form it takes, is a clash not so much of one civilization with another, but of civilization itself with forces that are utterly alien to it. Understanding that, I believe, will help us in our struggle against terrorism. It is in the spirit of that understanding that I have chosen to tell my story.

Vesselin Nedkov
Montreal, October 2003

1

MOSCOW

Tuesday, October 22, 2002   8:30 P.M.

Twenty-four hours before the events that changed my life forever, I was with friends strolling along Tverskaya Street, a broad concourse of glittering shops, hotels, and museums in the centre of Moscow. It was a special occasion. I was wrapping up my business affairs in Moscow after a three-year stint working for a Bulgarian forklift truck company. I had already moved to Canada with my wife, Petia, and had applied to take an MBA course at a Canadian university. I'd come back to Moscow for a few days to arrange for the last of my belongings to be shipped to Canada. It was, in a sense, my farewell trip to Russia, and I was in a celebratory mood.

We were walking past Pushkin Square, a favourite Moscow rendezvous, where a looming statue of the giant of Russian literature is now dwarfed by jumbo television screens, gigantic floodlit billboards,

1

and flashing neon signs. Tverskaya is one of the many spokes in a gigantic wheel that is Moscow, with the Kremlin at the hub. From the bright lights of Pushkin Square, it descends gently toward the forbidding red-brick watchtowers and golden cupolas that surround the Kremlin and Red Square, the heart of a city of twelve million people, encompassing just over one thousand square kilometres. It is the capital of a country that remains the largest on earth. The night air was cold but the snow had not yet come to muddy the streets and dampen our spirits.

I was born in Bulgaria, in a small town about three hundred kilometres east of the capital, Sofia. I had worked hard to obtain two degrees in business and had gone to work in Moscow upon graduating. Since the early 1990s, my dream had been to immigrate to Canada, where my brother, Nicolas, was already living and enjoying a successful career with a big telecommunications company. Petia and I had met at the economic university in Sofia and we were married in 2000. We finished the Canadian immigration process the same year, and while it took somewhat longer to clear the hurdles of red tape, everything had finally fallen into place. We became landed immigrants and found an apartment in Toronto. It seemed as though I would be accepted into an MBA program. My future had never looked brighter.

The first time I visited Moscow in the late 1980s, I was just a teenager. I had gone on an organized tour with the Pioneers, a state-run youth organization, and we travelled to Moscow on what the Russians called a "friendship train" in order to get to know Russians our own age. It was a standard form of cultural exchange in those days. One of my most vivid memories of that first visit was a conversation with the taxi driver who brought us from the train station to our billets. Out of the blue he asked if we had any bars of soap to sell. Why? I asked. Bulgarian soap was nothing special. If he'd asked us for something Bulgaria was famous for, like a bottle of attar of rose, or wine, we wouldn't have been surprised. "Soap is hard to get here," the taxi driver replied. He offered us five rubles for each bar of soap we had, and we took it. That was a lot of money in those days. I remember being slightly bewildered by this. Of course we all knew that many things were in short supply in Russia, more so than in Bulgaria. But this was Moscow, the capital of a huge empire that included my own country. How could there be a shortage of soap?

For a young boy from a small Bulgarian town, Moscow was an enchanting city, full of mystery. The streets and subways were always teeming with people, and the buildings seemed imposing and grand. Of course, looking back, I realize that compared with what it is now, it was a pretty bland, drab place, even in the era of Gorbachev and his famous programs of *glasnost* and *perestroika* that were meant to transform the country. Change was in the air, but the past still outweighed the present.

By the time I went to work there as an adult, in 1999, everything had completely changed. The Berlin Wall had come down when I was fourteen and a couple of years later the Soviet Union fell apart. After the failed coup in August 1991, the subsequent collapse of Communist rule and the Soviet Union, and the resignation of Mikhail Gorbachev as president, Procter and Gamble moved in to solve the soap problem and Moscow became the capital of a smaller country called the Russian Federation. It was still a huge, metropolitan city, but it was now changing so rapidly that it was impossible to keep track of things. In the late 1990s it was exciting to be asked by a Bulgarian company to work there.

My Russian had always been good, but part of my plan while in Moscow was to upgrade my English-language skills in preparation for my future move to Canada. I enrolled in a private language school called English First and began to study for my university entrance-level English exams. The class was sometimes taught by the school's academic director, Irina Filipova. Irina is a typical modern Muscovite, a professional woman who speaks several languages fluently and runs the language and teacher training programs at the school. Her English is excellent, and when she learned that I was preparing for my entrance exam, she offered to help me. She was a tough taskmaster and was certainly one of the reasons I passed with flying colours.

Irina was with us that evening as we walked through the streets, surrounded by the neon lights of the new Russia. Moscow seemed a fine place to be. Through the lens of my own good fortune it took on a Disney-like atmosphere, the ruby stars above the Kremlin scattered there as if from a magic wand. I was glad to be back briefly, glad to be with old friends for a few hours, but also eager to begin my new life in Canada.

As we passed a ticket kiosk near the underground shopping mall not far from the wall of the fortress, I had an impulse to thank Irina for her help by taking her to the theatre the following evening. While the others walked on, I ducked my head through the window of the kiosk. I asked the ticket agent, an elderly woman, what was currently playing in Moscow theatres, glancing over my shoulder to Irina for guidance. Nothing seemed to catch her fancy until, more out of cold and impatience than preference, Irina pointed to a large poster for the Russian musical *Nord-Ost*.

"I've always been curious about *Nord-Ost*," she said.

"Good. So have I," I responded, although to tell the truth, all I really knew about the play was that it was incredibly popular among young Muscovites, and that a life-sized plane landed on the stage during the second act.

"*Nord-Ost*? I have tickets for Wednesday, Thursday, and Friday," the ticket agent said.

"Is tomorrow evening okay with you?" I asked Irina. She nodded.

"Wednesday, October 23, it is then," the ticket agent responded. "If you take a seat at the end of the row in the orchestra, you'll pay a lot less, but since it's the middle of the week, you'll probably be able to move into better seats once the show starts."

The tickets cost the equivalent of about US$30 each. They were expensive by Moscow standards—you can get a good seat at the Bolshoi Theatre for far less—but I didn't mind. "You'll have great seats," the ticket agent said cheerily, "and when you're sitting pretty, you'll remember me."

I pocketed the tickets. Irina, who had been standing for some time waiting for the transaction to be completed, was now shivering. The temperature had dropped. It was the end of October and the full force of the Russian winter was about to descend.

Although I didn't know a lot about the play we were going to see, I couldn't help being aware of the eye-catching billboards for *Nord-Ost* that seemed to be all over Moscow, situated prominently along the wide, multi-laned arterial roads leading to the centre, or hanging from overpasses, where the millions of people who drove in and out of the city every day would see them. It was an impressive, Western-style advertising campaign that had put the name of the play into everyone's mind.

Nord-Ost was, in fact, one of a kind—a phenomenal Russian success story that had captured the public's imagination. By the time we bought our tickets, it had been running for more than a year, and hundreds of thousands of people had seen it. What was unique about *Nord-Ost* was that it was entirely Russian. It had Russian music, Russian choreography, Russian design, and, of course, a Russian cast. This was a homegrown mega-musical, something that had never been tried before in Russia. There was a lot to lose if it failed.

As we walked away from the ticket kiosk, we were accosted by a middle-aged man in a Russian army uniform bearing sergeants stripes. The soldier told me he was with a military unit that had returned from Chechnya. He held a loaf of bread in one hand, and he asked me for money to help him buy more food for his soldiers. It was not the usual beggar's story, and from what little I knew about the state of the Russian army, it was entirely believable. I dug into my pockets and gave him some rubles. He thanked me, then turned and walked away, toward Red Square.

We hurried to catch up with the others and find a bar to get warm, crossing Tverskaya Street, with its neon lights. The headlamps of shiny new cars reflected in the now wet streets, for it had started to rain. I didn't give the soldier a second thought. I was congratulating myself on having purchased tickets for the show. What better way to say farewell to Moscow than to see a play that represented, in a way, the new Russia? But Irina couldn't get the encounter with the poor soldier out of her mind. These men had risked their lives for their country and here they were, having to beg for food in the very shadow of the Kremlin.

2

CHECHNYA

Early October

Located on the southeastern peripheries of the Russian Federation, on the isthmus of land that separates the Black from the Caspian Seas, Chechnya is a landlocked territory of forbidding peaks and windswept valleys, ancient settlements and warrior tribes that for centuries have been at odds with themselves and with their Russian masters. It straddles the northern reaches of the Caucasus Mountains, with Dagestan to the east, Georgia and Ingushetia to the west, Azerbaijan to the south, and the vast plains of Russia to the north. Covering about sixteen thousand square kilometres, it is roughly the size of Northern Ireland and is home to one million people, the majority of whom live in the northern lowlands around the capital, Grozny. Most are of Chechen ethnicity, but there are many ethnic minorities, and a sizable Russian population as well, the result of at least two centuries of colonization. Grozny, in fact, began as a fortress town founded by the Russians, and its name, in Russian, means "terrible." Over the past ten years, as if fulfilling an awful prophecy, this city has become one of the most hideous places on earth.

Imagine a journey. It begins in Minutka Square in the centre of Grozny sometime in early October 2002. Once the site of a bustling market, this central intersection now lies in a war-ravaged moonscape of burnt-out buildings. The skeletal hulks of what were once apartment and office blocks loom over rubble and refuse. The standing ribs of the structures are blackened from the infernos that have swept through the interiors. The surroundings are reminiscent of the grotesque ruins of New York's World Trade Center. The analogy is apt, for Grozny has been literally blown apart by the terrorism of war, bombed and shelled by the Russian army, caught in the deadly crossfire of two ruthless forces that have been locked in a struggle to the death since the mid-1990s.

It is said that Chechen prisoners arriving at the Russian detention camp at Chernokozovo, north of Grozny, are greeted on arrival with a sign that says, "Welcome to hell." But in many ways, all of Chechnya is a hell on earth. People have been brutalized here in ways that defy imagination. Arbitrary arrest, torture, rape, and execution have become standard practice for the occupying Russian army. The Chechen rebels have kidnapped, extorted, tortured, and murdered in return. But in Minutka Square, in October 2002, life goes on. This is where the journey begins.

At the edges of the square, Chechen women have set up makeshift stalls and are attempting to sell whatever they can. Food and the other necessities of life are hard to come by here, but the women continue to engage in small-scale trading, buying and selling, bartering, carving out a bare existence from one day to the next. Around the square, children can be seen sorting through the rubble, looking for bricks and scrap metal to barter for bread, but there is so much unexploded ordnance buried in the debris that it becomes a horrific game of Russian roulette. At a truck dispensing fresh water, women line up with buckets to carry the water home. Grozny is often without running water and electricity for long periods. Some people live in bombed-out cellars, struggling to survive as best they can. Many of the women live alone, for the men have vanished, some simply made to disappear during the *zachistki,* the periodic sweeps or mopping-up operations conducted by the Russian army. Russian soldiers are everywhere.

Nearby, there is a pick-up point where you can catch a minibus from Grozny to towns in Dagestan. Each day, Chechen women board these buses, taking with them anything they think they can sell. At their destination they buy what supplies they can from the proceeds of these transactions and return with produce and other goods, which they then sell or barter for food in the markets in Grozny. Women traders are a familiar sight all over the Caucasus. Wearing traditional headscarves and ankle-length skirts, they trudge around lugging huge bags stuffed with wares. You can see them in the markets of Dagestan and Georgia and across the mountains in Azerbaijan. Many of them go farther afield. In the Dagestani town of Khasavyurt, you can board another minibus that will take you on the long, two-thousand-kilometre journey to Moscow.

In early October in Chechnya, people are already bundling up to protect themselves from the biting wind. In the mountains, the snows have come early. Grozny takes on an even grimmer appearance as the few remaining trees shed the last of their leaves. A group of six or seven women stands waiting by a bombed-out building for a bus to take them to Dagestan. Most of the women are older, seasoned traders, carrying plastic bags heavy with wares. But three of the waiting women are younger. They wear black headscarves in the Muslim style, long skirts, winter jackets, and muddy running shoes. They carry small bags and backpacks. One has a Walkman slung over her shoulder. The three young women are accompanied by a man. Apart from the driver, he will be the only male on the bus. One of these three women may be an actor at the National Theatre, another a professor of history at Chechen National University, and the third a famous Chechen athlete. What is almost certain is that, in this war, each has lost a brother, or a father, or a husband, or a child. They wait silently for the dilapidated bus to arrive. When it comes, they squeeze into a seat at the back, holding their bags on their laps.

Imagine the journey from Grozny to Khasavyurt. The bus rumbles along a potholed highway toward the border, past derelict farms and through villages ravaged by war—away from the mountains toward a different landscape. Every so often it stops at an army checkpoint, or *blokpost*. The passengers answer the soldiers' questions, their bags are checked, they give the soldiers money, and are waved on. The three women have enough rubles to see them through the thirty or so *blok-posti* that lie between Chechnya and Moscow. Moreover, their internal passports are in order. If suspicions are aroused, a few rubles will allay them. The bus crosses the border into Dagestan, the passengers disembark at Khasavyurt, a picturesque university town. Here they purchase tickets for Moscow. A few hours later they board another bus. This bus has two drivers. It will take them a couple of days to reach the Russian capital.

They leave Khasavyurt at night, driving due north out of Dagestan and heading toward Astrakhan and the Volga Delta. As day breaks they pass the vast oil fields in the alluvial wetlands, where the river spills its waters into the Caspian Sea. These are the largest oil deposits in Europe. The flares from the wells flicker against the morning sky as the bus approaches the industrial city of Astrakhan. Here the highway turns northwest and follows the Volga River, occasionally affording a view of the shipping lanes, the barges, and the tankers that ply this immense waterway through the heartland of Russia. The roads improve as they approach Volgograd, the city once called Stalingrad, now a sprawling industrial metropolis of over a million people, set at the confluence of the Volga and the Don Rivers. The bus weaves its way along the highway, now busy with trucks and rusty Ladas. Perhaps they stop at Volgograd to refuel and wash the bus windows, covered in grime after twelve hours on the road. The drivers switch places. They are deep inside Russia, and halfway to Moscow.

As they leave the city, perhaps they catch a glimpse of the memorial to those who died in the battle for Stalingrad in World War II, or the Great Patriotic War, as the Russians call it. It is the colossal figure of a woman warrior brandishing a sword that seems to pierce the heavens. This is Mother Russia, the goddess of patriotism and empire. She towers over the landscape, dwarfing everything in sight.

By this time the travellers have managed to negotiate perhaps fifteen or twenty *blokposti*. They are well on their way.

At night, most of the women sleep. As Russian towns flit by, the youngest, the one with the Walkman, listens to passages from the Koran. More roadblocks, more rubles. They drive through Borisoglebsk, where cupolas of ancient Orthodox churches preside over a nuclear weapons storage facility. Later they pass through Tambov, once summer home to both Tchaikovsky and Rachmaninov, a town studded with monuments to the dead—soldiers of the Great Patriotic War, victims of Stalin's oppression, heroes of the Afghan campaign. Compared with their homeland, the landscape here is flat, the highway lined by interminable stretches of forest, the towns enclaves of Soviet-style buildings and factories. The road widens again. Then, in the distance, the ramparts of Moscow's suburbs begin to take shape as kilometre after kilometre of dreary high-rise apartment buildings appear on the horizon. The highway becomes a broad, multi-laned motorway. They reach the outskirts of the city and are caught in the gridlock of the outermost ring road, the rim of the great wheel that encloses most of modern Moscow.

Finally, they arrive at their destination: the Luzniki Stadium, one of Moscow's largest sports facilities, where fleets of buses and trucks from the east disgorge their cargoes of passengers and produce arriving from all over the Caucasus, from Georgia and Azerbaijan, from Kazakhstan and Dagestan, from Ingushetia and Chechnya. They come in their thousands, bringing with them the smells and sounds and tastes of Caucasia and the East. The busy open-air market is teeming with people buying and selling. You can buy anything in Moscow's street markets, from cabbages to Gucci shoes. The markets are part of what makes Moscow exotic and diverse. And dangerous.

When the bus from Dagestan arrives at Luzniki, its occupants disembark and melt into the crowd. There is nothing noteworthy about them. They are simply three more Muslim women from Chechnya, come to trade in Moscow, come to visit family, come to escape the war.

But these women are different. They are three of about eighteen Chechen women who have been coming to Moscow in small groups since early October. They have all come with a single purpose. They have come to Moscow to die.

3

MOSCOW

Wednesday, October 23   5:00 P.M.

The day after we bought the tickets was one of those Moscow traffic days when it takes twice as long to get around the city than you expect. The weather was still cold and miserable. I had to visit business colleagues, then pick up some personal belongings and arrange for their transportation to Canada, and I was running late. I had rented a car and had planned, before picking Irina up from her workplace, to return to my friend's apartment, where I was staying, to change. In Moscow, theatre-goers dress up. But I was thwarted by the traffic, and the anticipation I'd felt the previous evening gradually gave way to frustration and impatience. Moscow is a city of hassles. The simplest tasks often seem almost impossible.

I was uncomfortable about going to the theatre in jeans and a leather jacket, and I was tempted to call the whole thing off. At one point, I reached for my cellphone but then realized that Irina would find this excuse lame and possibly rude. There was nothing to do but to stick to our original plan. I arrived late at the school to find that Irina had had a tiring day at work and had also been thinking of cancelling, but then decided against it. So we proceeded, both a little out of sorts, to the theatre.

By this time a wet snow was falling. Sludge splashed on the windscreen and made driving difficult. *Nord-Ost* was playing not in a conventional theatre in the centre but in what the Russians call a House of Culture in one of the older residential districts of Moscow, an area of low-rise apartment buildings about three kilometres south-east of the Kremlin. We had only a vague idea of where we were going, but traffic was by now flowing smoothly, so we followed the signs and found the theatre easily.

It would have been hard to miss. As we arrived at the intersection of Dubrovka and Melnikova Streets, there it was—a large, low building with a huge floodlit banner stretched across the façade declaring *"NORD-OST"* in big letters against a background of a blue sky filled with seagulls. The glass entranceway glowed invitingly in the cold evening. We turned onto Melnikova and from there into the parking lot, a large open plaza in front of the theatre that was beginning to fill with cars. A number of hardy skateboarders, oblivious to the weather and the gathering darkness, were taking a few last runs at a makeshift ramp they had set up at one end of the pavement. Beyond the plaza there was a park, with a cluster of trees and some benches. Irina and I got out of the car, opened our umbrellas against the wet snow, and made our way toward the theatre.

The House of Culture looks nothing like the large classical theatres found in the centre of Moscow. It's a sprawling, three-storey glass, concrete, and marble structure with a long façade facing Dubrovka Street, supported by large square pillars. The entranceway is a bank of glass doors sheltered by a long cement portico. It's a standard example of 1970s Soviet architecture, just as the mostly low-rise apartment buildings in the surrounding neighbourhood are typical of the housing built in the 1940s and '50s under Stalin. Without the huge blue banner, the fresh coat of white paint, and the spotlights, the House of Culture would have seemed like a relic from a bygone era. The most modern thing about it now, Irina remarked, was a gay club in the rear of the complex.

We walked up the three steps to the broad flagstone terrace in front of the theatre. It was getting close to curtain time, but people were still arriving, some on foot from the nearest Metro station almost a kilometre away. We made our way past a shady-looking scalper with a scruffy beard who tried to foist a pair of cut-rate tickets on us, then walked through the glass doors and into the brightly lit lobby.

In the warmth of the theatre, all the frustrations of the day seemed to fade. We checked our coats in the cloakroom that ran from one end of the ground floor to the other. It was staffed by students, their textbooks and school work set aside on chairs on the other side of the counter. Irina commented on their politeness: Moscow is not renowned for service with a smile. We looked around, lingering at a notice board covered with comments from playgoers, emotional thank-yous to the actors, and rave reviews, all testifying to the show's enormous popularity. People were arriving in groups—students, mothers with children, couples, friends, young professionals with their parents. It was clear that this was a family show, and that this was not the usual theatre-going Moscow crowd of members of the elite or the well-heeled nouveaux riches. Most of the people in this audience seemed to be university educated, professionals, people like us who had rushed from offices and classrooms to get there on time. I was relieved to see that my casual clothes were not inappropriate. Irina said she felt as though she were stealing this moment from her daily routine. There was still time before the play began, so we decided to look for something to eat.

The theatre was owned by a large industrial concern that manufactured ball bearings; the spacious lobby was dominated by a massive robot-like mannequin made entirely of enormous industrial-sized bearings and gigantic nuts and bolts. This heavy Soviet-era artifact stood in stark contrast to the airy lightness of the space, its square, mirrored pillars reflecting the lights in the high ceiling. At one end, a broad staircase led to a second-floor lobby where there were refreshment booths and a kiosk selling *Nord-Ost* memorabilia— soundtracks, T-shirts, pens, posters, toys, copies of *The Two Captains* (the novel on which the play was based), commemorative programs, and classier knick-knacks such as a shiny metal model of a sailing ship and leather pilots' bags, objects that symbolized the musical's themes. From here, an atrium rose to two upper levels, and if you climbed the staircase, it was possible to look down from a gallery on the top level onto the second-floor lobby. The rear wall of the top lobby was covered with a colourful Soviet-style ceramic mosaic depicting people at work, but that and the ball-bearing robot figure downstairs were the only reminder of the old days. A vast cycloramic canvas bearing the copy of an ancient celestial navigation chart hung on the ceiling and carried on down the front wall of the top lobby like a blue spinnaker sprinkled with stars, forming a dome overhead and covering the upper windows.

In the few minutes left before the curtain went up, we wandered back down to the concession booths on the second level, where teenaged kids in Pepsi T-shirts were selling wine and juices, pastries and sandwiches. Irina ordered a sandwich and a coffee and I ordered a juice. I was annoyed at having to pay forty rubles for such a small glass, but Irina argued that the price was justified, given the costs of renting the space, buying supplies, and paying the staff. It's a Broadway-style musical, she said. Why shouldn't there be Broadway prices? Such were our concerns at 6:50 P.M.

Irina told me that the play *Nord-Ost* was something of a cult among young people. It had its own fan club—mostly made up of teenagers and young adults—that organized special surprise events for the cast. For instance, on the evening of the one-hundredth performance, they had launched a hundred paper airplanes from the balcony. On the play's two-hundredth "anniversary," they unfurled a banner that quoted a line from the play: "If we are to be, let us be the best!" And on the three-hundredth performance, they brought in three hundred roses for the cast, arranged in the shape of a ship.

As we strolled around the lobbies, we were amazed at how much activity was going on in the building. As well as an auditorium, the House of Culture contained many smaller rooms, rehearsal halls, and dance studios. Children's dance classes and rehearsals for other shows were in full swing that evening. Many children were in the cast of the show—ten each night, but spread over several rotating casts—and before each performance, the children who were acting that night would warm up with voice and acting coaches. The building had also become a magnet for actors, and other theatre companies had rented rehearsal space in which to develop new projects. It felt good just to be there.

The *Nord-Ost* audience was summoned to their seats by the sonorous chimes of an electronic bell that sounded just like Big Ben—two warnings, then a final toll. We had seats in the rear section of the orchestra stalls. We entered the auditorium from the second-floor lobby, down a long sloping corridor, and then through a door that brought us to the back of the hall. On our way in we walked beside a young couple who appeared to be on their first date. In one hand, the girl was carrying a souvenir of the show—a teddy bear dressed like a pilot in goggles and cap. The boy had likely just bought it for her at the souvenir kiosk. In her other hand she held a bouquet of flowers.

We found our seats in the sixteenth row—seats two and three—but when the lights went down and we saw that no one had taken the seats to our right, we moved closer to the centre of the row. The house, with a capacity of twelve hundred, appeared to be about two-thirds full. There had been a lot of children in the lobby who had come with their parents to see the show; most of them seemed to be sitting in the balcony. As we settled into our seats, a woman's voice came over the PA system, reminding us to switch off our cellphones; Irina realized that she had left hers at home.

The lights dimmed, a hushed anticipation fell over the audience, and then, in the blackness, our ears were assaulted by the roar of an aircraft engine and, as it faded, the sound of waves crashing against rocks, and the cries of seagulls.

The curtain—really a series of grey sliding panels that resembled corrugated iron—parted to reveal a breathtaking set: six long ramps, each about one and a half metres wide, hinged on an elevated walkway at the back of the stage and operated by an automated system so they could be raised or lowered in any configuration, depending on the needs of the scene. A little boy was playing around some fishing boats set against a spectacularly lit backdrop meant to represent the subarctic sky near Archangelsk, in northern Russia.

The play's story was told entirely through song, with large ensemble choruses and dances, and it was presented with great verve and energy. But stripped of the song and dance, the story was a long way from Broadway; it was a real Russian epic. The boy, Sanya, who is mute, witnesses the brutal murder of a postman. When his father is wrongly accused of the deed, Sanya is unable to speak of what he has seen and his father is sentenced to death and executed. All Sanya has left is the postman's mailbag, which he took from the murder scene. He runs away to the city and is eventually taken in by a kindly mentor, who teaches him how to speak. He grows up and meets Katya, the daughter of an explorer who has gone missing in the Arctic and is assumed dead. The two teenagers fall in love. Sanya realizes that one of the letters in the dead postman's bag is from Katya's father to her mother, who has since remarried Katya's uncle. The letter reveals that the wicked uncle, now Katya's stepfather, had plotted to win her mother from her father by deliberately sending the expedition into the far north with inferior supplies and equipment so that they would all perish. Sanya tells what he knows, and Katya's mother is so overcome with guilt and remorse that she commits suicide. As the opening act ends, Sanya declares his determination to become a pilot and fly to the Arctic, find the remnants of the lost expedition, and uncover the truth that now lies hidden beneath the ice. The music swells to an emotional and thunderous climax. Sanya runs off the stage to wild applause.

In Russian theatres, intermissions are traditionally longer than is standard in the West. Playgoers promenade through the lobbies, savouring champagne and caviar, greeting their friends, discussing the program, chatting with each other. It is an opportunity to see and be seen. But at *Nord-Ost,* it was different. Families lined up for ice-cream cones and souvenirs. I ordered a glass of wine for Irina and juice for myself. The juice had a small fly floating in it; I felt a wave of irritation and demanded another.

We wandered up to the third floor, where there was an exhibition of children's art illustrating the *Nord-Ost* story. Then we went down to the ground floor, where we noticed that some people were leaving, mostly elderly couples complaining that the sound was too loud. We sat on a bench against the plate-glass windows and chatted. I have to admit that had I been alone, I might have been tempted to leave, but Irina was excited by the play, so I said nothing.

Irina saw *Nord-Ost* as more than just a cultural event. The musical had been the brainchild of two Russian singers, Georgi Vasilyev and Aleksei Ivaschenko, a popular duo that composed and performed its own songs. When the Communist system collapsed, Vasilyev discov- 'ered that he had a knack for business. In the early 1990s, he became involved in the cellphone revolution that was sweeping Central and Eastern Europe. Then in 1996, he began working on a project with a huge ambition: to change the face of Russian theatre. His first idea was to bring the mother of all mega-musicals—*Les Misérables*—to Moscow. He got in touch with the British impresario Cameron Mackintosh, the mastermind behind *Les Miz*. But in the end, Vasilyev and his Russian colleagues decided that rather than import a musical, they should write and produce one themselves.

And that's exactly what they did. They created a production company called Link. They put together a team of designers, admin- istrators, computer technologists, lighting technicians—five hundred people in all—and created a professional theatre operation big enough to handle the business and logistics of a major musical. They devel- oped the hardware and software for six separate computerized systems that could handle the special effects and scene changes. They put together a creative team of composers, arrangers, actors, dancers, and musicians to mount the play. Everyone knew how great a risk it was— not just financially, but artistically as well. If it failed, it would be a long time before anyone dared to try something similar again.

As we re-entered the auditorium, we were followed by a troupe of high-spirited children. They were the young actors who had appeared on stage in Act One, but instead of going home, here they were, piling in enthusiastically to see the second act. They sat down together in the vacant seats behind us.

The second act opened to the roar of an aircraft that seemed to be swooping from one side of the auditorium to the other, a sound so realistic that some people in the audience almost ducked for cover. The lights came up on the apron of the stage to reveal a group of young men dressed in World War II air-force tunics and tall, shiny boots. They were pilot cadets, and they were making good-natured fun of Sanya, who was meant to be piloting the aircraft buzzing overhead. The cadets were singing, their dance a boisterous combination of Cossack folk dancing and American tap. It was one of the show's hit numbers. Behind them, whirling lights like Roman candles, simulating rotating propellers, were projected onto the panels. The atmosphere was one of intense camaraderie and high spirits. The kids behind us were thoroughly enjoying themselves, yelling "Bravo" and singing along with the actors. We settled down to enjoy Act Two.

4

THE HOUSE OF CULTURE

Wednesday, October 23 9:05 P.M.

I first caught sight of the armed man out of the corner of my eye a few minutes into the second act. He was a shadow slipping into the theatre from a side entrance, then moving silently toward the stage and jumping lightly, almost soundlessly, onto the apron not far from where Irina and I were sitting. As he stood there in the semi-darkness, I could see that he was wearing new camouflage gear and that he had a Kalashnikov assault rifle slung over his right shoulder. But the most shocking thing about him was that he appeared to have no head.

For a moment, I thought he was part of the play. After all, the setting was military and the actors on stage were dressed in khaki tunics and tall, shiny boots, and there were the deafening sound effects of an aircraft roaring overhead. *Nord-Ost* was a show full of spectacu-lar special effects, surprises, and abrupt changes of mood. At some point, we were all expecting a full-sized plane to land on the stage before our eyes, as advertised. Why couldn't a sudden intrusion of an apparently headless gunman be part of the action?

The man scanned the audience, as though looking for someone, and I now saw why he seemed headless: he was wearing a black ski mask. Could he be with the Special Forces, a Russian emergency rapid response force? Perhaps he was checking out a tip-off—a bomb threat or a report that a fugitive was hiding among the audience. Such things happen in Russia. At any moment, I thought, he'd leap off the stage, drag a man out of his seat, and arrest him.

Instead, the man moved quickly to the centre of the stage, firing a volley of shots into the air. The performers stopped dancing. The musicians in the orchestra pit, who couldn't see what was going on, thought that the actors had missed their cue and repeated the same phrase—over and over. A second masked man came from the opposite wing and the two men hustled the actors off the stage and into the audience, yelling at them to sit down and shut up. A few people in the audience actually applauded, and one woman said later that she had been impressed, at first, at how convincingly the performers had expressed fear and horror.

While this was going on, a man slipped into an empty seat beside me. He had a black beard and dark curly hair, and he was wearing a white suit that shone unnaturally in the gloom. I turned to him and asked, "Is this for real?"

The man didn't reply. He didn't even look at me; he merely shrugged.

I know the AK-47 well. I trained with it when I was doing my stint in the Bulgarian army, and I became a pretty good shot. I know the distinctive sound it makes, and the sound this gun had made didn't seem right: it was a dull, dead, almost hollow sound, not the sharp crack I was used to. At first I was sure the man had fired blanks. Then I looked up at the ceiling. I could see pockmarks; bits of plaster had come loose and were falling down through the shafts of light. These were real bullets. I glanced at the man next to me, who was still looking straight ahead, not saying a word. I decided not to speak to him again.

Other armed men, about thirty or forty of them, started pouring into the theatre, moving rapidly along the aisles in the semi-darkness, spreading out around the audience, and in the balcony, too, men in camouflage and masks. But more shocking than the men were the women who were with them. There were eighteen of them, and they wore dark clothes, padded jackets, trousers, and high boots. Their faces were hidden behind black shawls wrapped around their heads so that only their eyes showed. They were carrying grenades and each of them was armed with a pistol. They quickly took up positions at regular intervals around the perimeter of the audience. The jarring and terrifying presence of these women was what finally convinced me that the situation was utterly real. Nor was I alone. I felt the frozen, silent horror of the eight hundred others in the auditorium. Irina clutched my arm, too afraid to speak.

One of the men on stage shouted for our attention: "We are from Chechnya," he yelled in accented Russian, brandishing his Kalashnikov. "A war is going on there. We've just brought that war to Moscow!"

It was a strange moment, like losing control of a car. Everything is suddenly in slow motion as you watch yourself helplessly spin off the road. You're too mesmerized to feel anything at first. And that was how it was now. Everyone—even the children—must have known we were in trouble, but no one knew yet just how serious. There was no apparent panic, just a shocked silence as the musicians, who had finally realized that something was wrong, stopped playing. The single note of a violin lingered in the air like a tiny scream. I looked at Irina. She was staring intently at the men on the stage. Later, she said it felt as though she were being wrenched violently out of one unreality and plunged into another. One minute, you're watching a play, caught up in the spectacle and the story, wondering if the young hero is going to realize his dream, find the truth, win back the woman he loves. The next minute, you're a hostage in the middle of a real war being waged two thousand kilometres away.

It was dark inside the theatre. The house lights were off, and the only illumination came from the stage. The spotlights projected onto the sliding panels to represent airplane propellers were still on, flickering ominously into the dark auditorium. I could feel an odd rumbling sensation, as if a Metro train were passing beneath the theatre. Then I realized what it was: the row of seats was shaking. People were trembling with fear.

Meanwhile, at the back of the hall, other armed terrorists were herding people at gunpoint into the theatre from the lobbies and the administrative offices. There were young students wearing uniform-like smocks over their street clothes—kids I recognized from the cloak-room and the concession booth in the lobby upstairs. Others were probably box office staff and theatre administrators, workers who had stayed late and were trapped when the terrorists burst through the front doors and began sweeping people in front of them as they moved deeper into the building. The hostages were walked down the aisles at gunpoint and then ushered into empty seats by the women terrorists.

The terrorists also brought in groups of children who had been rehearsing elsewhere in the building. The man in the white suit sitting beside me may have been waiting in the lounge when the terrorists rushed in and was likely one of the first they pushed into the theatre. Perhaps he was a father waiting to pick up a son or daughter after the show. If so, he had probably been too terrified to answer my question.

For the next hour, the terrorists worked quickly and efficiently, moving rapidly through the gloom, preparing the theatre for the siege they knew would come. They worked as though they were familiar with the task, as though they had done this kind of thing before.

Some of the men dragged in, from the wings, large canvas bags, the kind athletes use to keep their gear in. They put the bags in the middle of the stage, then started unloading packages and handing them out to the women. Most of the packages were long, flat bundles the size of a large fanny pack, wrapped in transparent plastic sheeting. I watched with horrified fascination as the women fastened them with tape to big Russian military belts, then buckled the belts around their waists. The packages were clearly homemade bombs, stuffed with small pieces of metal—mostly nails and ball bearings—that would turn into a hail of lethal projectiles if the bombs went off. Two wires protruded from each pack, and the women held these in one hand. I knew enough about explosives to know that, so far, they didn't have the means to detonate the bombs. Once they did, though, all they had to do was touch a battery to the two wires. The bomb would explode, killing the bomber and everyone else in range. Although none of the women seemed to have batteries as yet, each carried not just a pistol but also a hand grenade with the safety ring around one of her fingers. If she were to relax her grip, the grenade would fall from her hand, the weight of it would pull out the pin, exploding the grenade, which could, in turn, detonate the bomb. Even if the women were shot before they could touch off the explosives, they could still, in death, turn into horrific human bombs.

While the women were rigging themselves up, the men were laying booby traps and attaching explosive devices to the walls. Moving methodically along the aisles and using long strips of wide sticky tape, they affixed more of the homemade bombs to the wall at regular intervals, then connected them with wires so all could be detonated at once. For a long time, intermittently interrupted by the sound of gunfire and breaking glass coming from the front of the building, we could hear the loud *skriiiitch* as lengths of tape were torn off the roll, a sound as unnerving as fingernails being scraped across a blackboard.

Sometimes the men would shout at each other in Chechen. At other times, one would yell, *"Allahu akhbar!"*—"God is great!"—and the others would stop what they were doing, stand upright and still, close their eyes, and repeat the cry loudly three times. It confirmed what I was already beginning to suspect: these people were more than Chechen nationalists; they were quite possibly also religious fanatics.

After about a half hour, two men moved to the front of the theatre and stood on the floor close to the stage, their AK-47s cocked on their hips. Neither wore masks. One of them, whom I learned later was Movsar Barayev, the leader of the group, was in his mid-twenties, with a thin face and expressionless eyes. He wore a dark wool cap with the rim turned up. He said something in Chechen. Perhaps he was asking if there was anyone from Chechnya in the audience, because the next thing he said was in Russian: "Is anyone here from Georgia or Azerbaijan or . . ." He hesitated, as though he didn't want to run through a whole list, and then added, almost as an afterthought, "Are there any Muslims here?"

At first, no one moved. It wasn't clear why the terrorists were asking this question, or what would happen to people who so identified themselves. Then a few people came forward and were led out of the auditorium. (I later discovered that there were other Muslims in the audience who chose to stay.) Almost at the same time, the terrorist I would come to know as Yassir asked quietly for any foreigners among the hostages to come forward. I quickly asked Irina if she thought I should admit to being a foreigner. I had my Bulgarian passport and my Canadian landing papers with me. Since we thought they'd find out sooner or later, we decided it would be best to admit it now. I got out of my seat, edged my way to the aisle, walked up to the man, and showed him my passport.

Yassir was clean-shaven with a broad face, brown eyes, dark hair and—paradoxically—a demeanour that made him seem at first more approachable than some of the other terrorists. I opened the passport for him and took out my landing papers, which were folded inside. "I'm Bulgarian," I said in Russian, "but I live in Canada."

He examined the passport and the landing papers slowly, deliberately taking his time. "Okay," he said at last, handing me back my passport. "Go and sit in the back row. We're going to release you." He pointed to the seats near the left-hand entrance to the theatre. I could scarcely believe my luck. But as I walked back to my seat, I realized that I couldn't leave Irina alone in this. I sat down beside her and asked if she had her ID booklet with her. She rummaged in her handbag, then whispered that she must have forgotten it at home. She was worried, but I was relieved. It would make the whole charade that was beginning to take shape in my mind a lot easier.

Without explaining anything to her, I took her by the hand, cautioned her to speak only in English, and led her along the row and down the aisle. Yassir was still there, talking to other foreigners.

When our turn came to speak to Yassir again, I said, almost as if I were introducing her to an acquaintance, "This is my wife. She's Canadian."

He looked at her intently for what seemed like a long time, and my heart sank. I was sure he didn't believe me.

"Her passport," he said.

"The police have it," I replied. "She just arrived a few days ago, and she had to register with the police and they haven't given it back yet." I was hoping he hadn't noticed, or wouldn't remember, that the entry stamp in my passport was dated a couple of weeks earlier. But I had a story ready for that one too—that she'd come over to join me for the last few days of my business trip.

"She doesn't understand Russian," I added, hoping that would discourage him from trying to talk to her.

Yassir looked nonplussed, as though this was a problem beyond his authority to resolve. He looked around, and I thought he was going to seek advice from someone else. What if I had made a terrible mistake that would cost us both dearly? Then I heard Irina's voice.

"What's going on?" she asked in English.

Both Yassir and I looked at her. She was smiling, as though she didn't understand how serious things were, but I could feel her hand trembling. Trying to smile, I repeated in English what I'd said in Russian, while Yassir looked on with some interest. My mouth was suddenly very dry.

"Doesn't she understand Russian at all?" he asked.

"No," I said. "Not a word."

He paused. "Okay," he said at last. "Go to the back row."

We retrieved Irina's purse and as we walked up the aisle, one of the women standing guard nearby demanded to know where we were going. I pointed back at Yassir, who was still dealing with the people lined up at the front. "He told us to move to the back. We are foreigners." That seemed to satisfy her and, with her gun, she gestured for us to pass.

The seats at the back of the theatre were empty. That we had been sent here I took as an encouraging sign. If the terrorists were intending to let us go, it made sense to gather all the foreigners in one place, close to the exit and as far away as possible from the other hostages. But then the back rows began to fill up as more people were brought into the auditorium. Irina and I deliberately took seats as close as possible to the end of the row; as new people arrived, we stood to let them pass. I felt more secure there: if we were stuck in the middle when shooting started, we'd have no means of escape, nowhere to go except under the seats. At the end of the row, at least we could try to run for it. However, our position also put us practically in the lap of one of the women suicide bombers. If she blew herself up, we'd certainly die along with her. It made no sense to want to sit at the end, but then, nothing was making much sense, so I followed my instincts.

I looked at my watch. Though not much more than half an hour had elapsed since the terrorists had taken over the theatre, it seemed much longer. They were still fixing explosives to the back wall; from our new seats, the chilling sound of tape being ripped off the spool was louder now. Yassir, apparently having finished separating the foreign from the domestic hostages, now sat a few rows in front of us on the backs of one of the seats, facing us, trying to stare us down, leering and waving his gun in our direction, clearly enjoying his absolute power over us. When one of the hostages tried to ask him something, he shot back, "Don't address us! Address the sisters!"

The "sisters" were now being given nine-volt batteries, the kind with male-female connectors at the top and that are commonly used for small devices such as smoke detectors and radios. These batteries they taped to their belts, fastening the opposite connectors, which fit into the battery connectors, to the ends of the wires leading from the bombs strapped around their waists. All that each of the women had to do now to kill herself and us was fit the connector in her left hand into the battery top. It was primitive and simple, but I knew it would work. As I watched the women put the finishing touches on their lethal hardware, I started to study them more closely. They were mostly young, though the woman sitting on a chair nearest to us seemed older and had some kind of authority over the others. She seemed approachable, and so I asked her why they were doing this.

Her response was all the more chilling for being delivered in a flat, emotionless voice: "We are ready to die," she said. "We want to die more than you want to live."

5

CHECHNYA

To understand why someone from Chechnya might be willing to die for their cause, you need to look at Chechen history.

Chechen history is tortured and bloody and unremittingly violent. For centuries, the Russians have tried to pacify the region. For centuries, the Chechens have fought back with a ferocity that defies understanding. Their oppressors have long considered the Chechens savage and primitive, not unlike the way some governments in the Western Hemisphere regarded the Native peoples within their jurisdictions, and yet they have fought against the Chechens using methods that have undermined their own claim to be a civilized nation. "The only good Chechen is a dead Chechen," a phrase said to have been coined by a nineteenth-century Russian general, Alexei Yermolov, predates American General Philip Sheridan's more famous dictum, "The only good Indian is a dead Indian" by about half a century. The Chechens, for their part, have despised the Russians and retaliated in kind.

Warring tribes and feuding clans had subsisted in the region for thousands of years, but it was only in their clashes with the Russians, and their adoption of a Sufi form of Islam, that the Chechens began, around the early nineteenth century, to emerge as a distinct nationality in the modern sense. Sufism is considered a mystical form of Islam. Its adherents perform dance rituals and meditation and, since the nineteenth century, have been at odds with followers of the more conservative forms of Islam that emerged in the Middle East.

In the late eighteenth century, a Sufi leader, Sheik Mansur, led a struggle against Czarist Russia in an effort to create a single Islamic state in the Caucasus. He was defeated, but not before he had managed, temporarily, to establish an emirate that embraced parts of Chechnya and neighbouring Dagestan. His struggle was taken up in the following century by a succession of leaders, most notably Imam Shamil, who is still either revered or reviled today as the real founder of the modern Chechen nation. Shamil's prowess as a military commander helped create the myth of Chechen invincibility and deepened the traditions of a warrior culture that many Chechens still profess to live by. He was something like the Rob Roy of Chechnya and proved a tenacious opponent. Twice in the course of bloody campaigns against the Russian armies, he managed almost magically to elude his opponents and then re-emerged to turn what looked like certain disaster into victory. Shamil ultimately surrendered in 1859, but to defeat him the Russians had to deploy over three hundred thousand troops, more than one-third of their standing army at the time.

In the periods of relative peace between battles, Shamil had managed to set up a rudimentary system of local government that created a quasi-modern country out of an anarchic assembly of clans.

He based his rule on Islamic law, though it was ultimately backed by his own personal authority, which he believed needed reinforcing by heavy-handed acts of repression, sometimes involving hostage-taking. Shamil's cruelties divided even the Chechens and, to this day, there are some who would never dream of calling their offspring Shamil, though it remains a popular first name in the territory.

Between Imam Shamil's defeat and the Russian Revolution in 1917, the Chechens rose against the Russians many times, and during the post-revolutionary Civil War period, from 1917 until 1925, the Chechens fought against both the Red and the White Russian armies. One of the principal warlords, a Sufi leader named Ujun Haji, refused to distinguish between the Czarists and the Communists. They were all Russians, and therefore the enemy. "I am weaving a rope," he is reported to have said, "to hang engineers, students, and, in general, all those who write from left to right."

Under Joseph Stalin, who was himself from neighbouring Georgia and therefore could be presumed to know the region and share an affinity with its people, the Chechens were finally absorbed, uneasily, into the Soviet Union, along with the other North Caucasian ethnic groups. The Soviet Mountain Republic, established in 1921 to include the Chechens and their closest neighbours, was broken up in 1925 into individual autonomous regions. In 1936, Stalin lumped the Chechens together with the neighbouring Ingush in what was called the Chechen-Ingush Autonomous Socialist Republic. Administratively it was never a full Soviet republic; instead it was made part of the Russian Republic. This status meant relatively little while the Soviet Union lasted, but it had enormous consequences for the Chechens and the Ingush when the USSR finally collapsed in 1991. It meant that while other full Soviet republics, like Ukraine or Georgia, attained their independence with relative ease, the Russians were unwilling to let go of a region that they considered part of the body of mother Russia.

During World War II, some Chechens are said to have fought alongside the Nazis against the Russians, and after the Germans were routed at Stalingrad in 1943, Stalin moved to implement a final solution to the problem of the recalcitrant, disloyal Caucasian nationalities. The following year, with characteristic ruthlessness, he deported the entire Chechen nation, along with five other nationalities in the North Caucasus region—more than a million people in all—to resettlement camps in Kazakhstan, in Central Asia.

Astonishingly, Stalin did this without prior notice and virtually overnight. In "Operation Mountaineer," as it was innocuously called, tens of thousands of troops from the NKVD—the dreaded Soviet secret police at the time—descended on the region. They rounded up half a million Chechens and Ingushes and began moving them out the same day in cattle trucks and trains, allowing them only twenty kilograms of luggage each. In mountain villages where there was no adequate transport in the middle of winter, the people were simply slaughtered. In Khaibakh, for instance, seven hundred people—the elderly, the sick, children, and pregnant women—were locked in a barn and burned to death. Patients in hospitals were murdered in their beds. According to the most conservative estimates, in addition to the thousands summarily executed on the spot, seventy-eight thousand Chechens died from starvation or cold on the one-thousand-kilometre journey to the Gulags of Kazakhstan. Other estimates suggest that as many as one-third of the population of Ingushetia-Chechnya—well over two hundred and fifty thousand people—lost their lives as a result of the deportation.

And then, somewhere in Moscow, a real-life precursor of Winston Smith, the protagonist of George Orwell's *Nineteen Eighty-Four*, began the task of excising the memory of the rebellious, unsubmissive peoples of the Northern Caucasus from history books, encyclopedias, and school textbooks. The intention, it seems, was to make them vanish from the face of the earth without a trace.

This did not happen. In exile, the Chechens distinguished themselves by their defiance—not just individual Chechens but, as
Alexander Solzhenitsyn writes in his history of the Gulag system, "the
whole nation to a man." Chechen workers refused to be deferential to
their bosses. Chechen parents refused to send their children to the
local schools. The men sought out jobs as drivers—jobs that would
give them a modicum of dignity and, as Solzhenitsyn points out with
barely disguised admiration—opportunities to steal. The Chechens
stole relentlessly and shamelessly from Kazakhs and Russians alike,
apparently considering it almost a birthright. "And here is the
extraordinary thing," Solzhenytsin writes. "Everyone was afraid of
them. No one could stop them from living as they did. The [Soviet]
regime which had ruled the land for thirty years could not force them
to respect its laws. . . . The Chechens walk the Kazakh land with
insolence in their eyes, shouldering people aside, and the 'masters of
the land' and non-masters alike make way for them." Clearly, these
were not a people who gave up easily.

In 1956, when Nikita Krushchev began his tentative unmasking of
some of Stalin's crimes, the Chechens were among the first of the
exiled peoples to take advantage of the thaw. Even before Krushchev
began officially permitting the North Caucasians to return to their
ancestral lands, many Chechens had already begun bribing their way
back, and by 1957 they were moving back to Chechnya in large
numbers. Not surprisingly, they proved adept at "persuading" the
interlopers—Russians who had occupied their homes and proper-
ties—to leave. "The Russians began to leave as soon as we came back,"
one Chechen said. "They seemed to be afraid of us . . . most slipped
away in the night, and the local authorities lent them lorries. Within
a few months, they had all gone."

But the Russians hadn't all gone. The Chechen-Ingush Autonomous
Socialist Republic picked up where it had left off—a region where

Russian, not Chechen, was the language of administration and education, and where most of the top positions in government were held by
Russians. Still, the Chechens' entrepreneurial skills enabled many of
them to become relatively wealthy very quickly, and by the mid-1970s,
according to some witnesses, they had the upper hand in Chechnya,
much as the Mafia had in Sicily. The Chechens had also managed to
establish strong criminal gangs in Moscow itself, with an influence
that extended into some of the main Soviet government ministries. By
the time Mikhail Gorbachev came to power in 1985, Chechens were
once again the major economic and social force in Chechnya, though
the Russians still controlled their political and cultural life.

By 1989, the year the Soviet empire began to crumble, Chechnya
was the most ethnically homogeneous province in the North
Caucasus, with about eight hundred thousand Chechens out of a total
population of over a million. It also had the strongest economy in the
region, based on oil and manufacturing. By the end of 1989, pressured
by a wave of peaceful revolts in Eastern Europe, the Soviets surrendered control of virtually all satellite states in that region and, two
years later, in 1991, following an attempted coup against Gorbachev,
the Soviet Union began dismantling itself. But still, Russia kept
Chechnya firmly in its grasp.

Led by Jokhar Dudayev, a former Soviet general, the Chechens
began to take steps to extricate themselves from the administrative
ties that bound them to Russia. On November 1, 1991, five days
after being elected president of the Chechen Republic, Dudayev
formally declared unilateral independence. This did not sit well with
the Russians. The new Russian president, Boris Yeltsin, declared a
state of emergency in the area. Little more than a month later, on
December 12, 1991, the Soviet Union ceased to exist, and was
succeeded, in law, by the new Russian Federation. Clumsy attempts
were made in 1992 and 1993 to regularize relations between the new

federation and the self-proclaimed independent Chechen state—Dudayev, apparently, would have been content with some kind of confederal arrangement with Russia—but nothing came of them. Neither the Russians nor any other country recognized Chechnya's new status, and the Russian leaders were too preoccupied with their own problems to pay serious attention to the issue.

The brief period of Chechen autonomy was hardly a golden age of peace and tranquility. From the moment they declared their independence, Dudayev's government was barely able to assert its authority. Moreover, a large part of the Chechen economy was based on crime and trafficking in arms and drugs. What legitimate industries there were, like the extraction, refinement, and shipment of oil, were largely controlled and managed by Russians. The irony was that the Chechen gangs running outlaw "businesses" had, as their main clients, large Russian institutions—the army, the banks, the government. This is one reason why the picture of Russian-Chechen relations is so murky and hard to interpret: such hidden connections are almost impossible to monitor, let alone assess. Even in its quasi-independence, Chechnya was bound to Russia by invisible, underground filaments that could scarcely be disrupted or regularized by politicians. Though politicians may have held the visible, constitutional reins of power, they could not govern the forces that were really in control: the armies, the security organizations, and the gangs that ran the smuggling rackets, the kidnapping schemes, and the black markets. In other words, they had little control over the very elements in any society that thrive on war, profit from it, and therefore promote it.

It was, and remains, a recipe for permanent conflict, the kind that eventually drives people to desperate measures.

6

THE HOUSE OF CULTURE

Wednesday, October 23   10:00 P.M.

The terrorists now began lugging in three large, heavy canisters that I recognized as gas tanks salvaged from Soviet-era trucks. These, too, were homemade bombs. Inside each canister was a huge artillery shell with a detonator. The space around it was packed with screws, nails, ball bearings, and pieces of scrap metal that would kill anyone within range. The terrorists put one of the bombs in the centre of the auditorium, about seventeen rows from the front, and another in the middle of the balcony, where some of the audience was also being held captive. The third bomb was placed in the middle of the stage.

The Chechens had positioned the bombs so that if they all went off at once, every one of us would be caught in a crossfire of deadly shrapnel and the building itself would probably be brought down.

One way or another, we would all be dead, including the terrorists and anyone trying to rescue us.

The odd thing was, I don't remember feeling any panic. Instead, I became hyper-alert. My mind was working on its own, watching the terrorists, observing, calculating, assessing, looking for clues, hypothesizing about what they might or might not be capable of. Some of the male terrorists kept their ski masks on; others took them off. Did this mean that some thought they might survive, while others, certain that they would die, no longer cared if anyone knew what they looked like? When the women first came in, some of them had clustered around a group of the men near the front, not far from where Irina and I were sitting, and they introduced themselves to the men as though they had never met before. Was this the first time this band of terrorists had ever been together? Had they all come to Moscow separately and met only tonight, inside the theatre? Might they not be as cohesive or as well trained as they seemed? Or were they in fact less predictable and therefore more dangerous?

And how had such a large group managed to get inside the theatre without attracting attention? Had the men come in civilian clothes, changing into their camouflage uniforms and masks once they were inside? Had some of them been in the audience during the first act? And what about the women? Had they too been dressed in civilian clothes, perhaps waiting in the small park in front of the theatre, putting on the Islamic dress just before they entered the theatre? Were they noticed entering the theatre, and were the authorities already aware—before the gunfire that may have alerted them—that something was going on in the House of Culture? Who were their leaders? Was it Movsar Barayev, the man who had jumped up on the stage first? Or Yassir, the man who had looked at my passport? Were there others, behind the scenes, who had yet to reveal themselves? Might there even be a single mastermind behind this, an invisible leader calling the shots from a safe distance?

At about 10 P.M., one of the Chechen women turned on a transistor radio and tried to find a station broadcasting the news. The terrorists had been talking among themselves, and though I couldn't understand what they were saying, it was clear they were curious to know whether word of the hostage-taking had gotten out. The woman fiddled with the dial, and when she finally found one of the major stations, it was playing music. She turned up the volume, then held up the radio almost gleefully. "You see?" she said. "There's nothing about us on the radio! Your government doesn't care about you!"

But she kept searching, and finally she found a station that was broadcasting a special bulletin. We listened carefully, but all it said was that a group from the Caucasus region were holding about forty or fifty people hostage at the House of Culture on Dubrovka Street. The woman couldn't contain herself. "Listen to this!" she shouted to another Chechen woman in the back row. "Forty or fifty people!" She laughed, then addressed the theatre: "Look, people," she shouted, "there's just forty or fifty of you!"

What were we—all eight hundred of us—supposed to think? To me, this probably meant that it was too early for the authorities to have properly assessed the situation. But did the authorities really believe there were only forty or fifty hostages inside? Were they so poorly informed, or were they deliberately broadcasting misinformation that diminished the magnitude of the event? Then again, maybe the women hadn't heard the report properly: maybe it had said forty or fifty *hostage-takers*. By my rough count, that was about the number of terrorists in the theatre.

The Chechen men were still setting up bombs and detonators throughout the theatre when a terrible commotion broke out behind us. Everyone looked around in alarm. At the rear of the auditorium was a control room with a glass window set in the wall so those inside could see the stage. One of the terrorists, eager to break into the control room, started pounding on the glass with the butt of his rifle.

He made a lot of noise, but when the glass didn't yield he grew angrier; finally, it was clear that he was getting ready to shoot the window out. What if the glass were bulletproof and the bullets ricocheted back and killed some of us, or we were injured by flying glass?

He cocked his gun and one of the women suicide bombers, seeing what was about to happen, told us to bend down and protect our heads with our hands. Just then, another male terrorist came up and pushed the other terrorist's gun aside, shouting at him in Chechen. At the same time, we could hear the sound of shooting; it was outside the auditorium, but still inside the building. The terrorists were yelling and again there was the sound of breaking glass. Some of the hostages began screaming. Had an attack already started? Instinctively, we crouched on the floor under the seats, and we remained there for some time.

I wasn't sure what time it was when Movsar moved to the front of the theatre, just by the orchestra pit. One of the terrorists had asked for my wristwatch. It was a good watch, but I didn't think it was wise to refuse. By now, the terrorists had found the control panel for the house lights, so the auditorium was brighter and we could see what was happening at the front. Movsar stood there for a moment, then said, "Have the small children come up here to me."

A ripple of panic went through the audience. There were several children on the main floor and many more in the balcony, some quite young, some in their teens.

"What do you mean by small?" one of the parents cried out.

"Only kids under the age of twelve," Movsar replied. "In Chechnya, when a boy is twelve, he has to be a soldier, and you Russians treat him as a man. Why should your children be any different?"

At first, the parents and the minders were afraid to let the children leave their sides. But they started trickling forward, until there was a long line of kids standing in front of the stage, trembling, frightened, and tired, some rubbing their eyes, some crying and looking desperately back at their parents for guidance, the armed, masked men towering over them. A few of the children tried to follow their parents back to their seats. By this time the parents must have realized that the terrorists intended to release the children, but that didn't make leaving them alone at the front of the theatre any easier. I heard a man tell a young girl not to stop at the cloakroom for her coat but to go straight to the Metro.

One mother, when she realized that the children were about to be released, pushed her daughter to the front, even though the girl desperately wanted to stay with her. Both were crying. Movsar lost patience and sent them back to their seats. "All right, all right," he said. "Forget it. That's all. We're not going to release anyone else." But when the friend of a woman who was seven or eight months pregnant came to the front and pleaded with him for her release, he relented. Astonishingly, the audience burst into applause.

The terrorists led the children up the side aisle, past where we were sitting, and into the upper-level foyer. Then they were made to go down the stairs and into the main lobby unaccompanied. The terrorists would have known that the Russian Special Forces had sharpshooters positioned around the theatre who could easily pick off any terrorist who came into view in the glass entranceway. The line of children left the auditorium and we followed them in our mind's eye as they disappeared into the lobby—so recently filled with strolling families enjoying an ice cream at intermission, with couples holding hands and buying CDs, with students serving wine and dainty sandwiches. It was now a dangerous no-man's land in a war zone. The theatre was silent as we listened, hoping against hope that there would be no gunfire. Several minutes passed. Nothing. You could feel the relief in the air. The children had managed to get out safely.

Meanwhile, more and more people had been brought into the auditorium from elsewhere in the building. One of them was a tall man about thirty years old, with long, ginger-coloured hair swept back in a ponytail and a self-assured demeanour. His name was Igor, and he directed an Irish-dancing troupe that rehearsed several nights a week in the theatre. Along with him came about thirty of the dancers, most of them young girls in tights, dressed for practice. They filed into the rows ahead of us, and Igor took the aisle seat, as if to protect them from what might come from that direction. The young dancers were terrified, but Igor talked calmly and confidently to them, as though no harm could come to them as long as he was there.

Next, an elderly man with thick glasses and a red scarf was brought in and corralled into one of the rows. He was wearing a shabby brown leather jacket and a cap. The big plastic bag he carried appeared to be stuffed with newspapers and books and odd bits of clothing. There was something comic about him, something naïve, as though he had just awakened from a dream and had blundered into the theatre without really knowing where he was, or what was happening there. He talked to the terrorists in a loud, penetrating voice, treating them as a minor annoyance that could simply be swept aside. I wondered if he was slightly mad. "Okay, guys," the old man said, "that's enough. I'm going home." And he got out of his chair, gathered his belongings, and managed to get out of the row and start moving toward the exit.

"Where do you think you're going?" one of the terrorists yelled at him.

"I told you, I'm getting out of here," the man said, as though the question had been one that required an answer.

"Get back to your place or I'll shoot you," the terrorist yelled.

The old man turned to face him. "Look, I'm seventy-five," he said. "Go ahead and shoot me."

For a moment, the two of them glared at each other, and I didn't know which one would back down first. The man might have been a World War II veteran or a prisoner in the Gulag and, if so, he had seen so many horrible things that nothing could frighten him—not even a masked man in army fatigues threatening to shoot him. Perhaps he was simply drunk and didn't care. Several people close to him stood up. "Don't make trouble. Go back to your seat!" they said.

The man looked around, as though realizing for the first time that he wasn't alone. Then, slowly, he went back to his row, sat down, and pulled out a newspaper, which looked old and yellow and out of date, and, with his bag on his knees, he started to read, just as he might have done if he were on a park bench or waiting for a train.

I had already talked to the woman in the aisle at the end of our row about where she and the other hostage-takers were from and what their demands were. But she would say no more than that they were from Chechnya, and that they wanted the war there to end. When I pushed her for details, all she would say was: "Our commander is going to talk to you in a little while. He'll tell you. Watch the stage," she said. Then she added cryptically: "The main event is going to happen on the stage."

"Why us?" one Russian woman asked. "We've come to the theatre to have fun. Why do you think we can do anything about the war in Chechnya? We're just ordinary people."

"We have to live every day with this war," the Chechen woman replied, "while you are here, laughing and having a good time. When you go home, you'll go home to your own beds. You'll be safe, your husbands and children are safe. Why didn't you go to Red Square, to demonstrate against the war in Chechnya? It was the least you could have done, and you didn't even do that. So shut up, and stop complaining. This is nothing."

7

CHECHNYA

1994–2002

In hindsight, the slide into open warfare between Russia and Chechnya seems inevitable. The Chechen leader, Jokhar Dudayev, may have been impulsive and unpredictable, and Russian president Boris Yeltsin may have been an alcoholic misled by unscrupulous, manipulative advisers, but in the end, the quality of their leadership was less important than the fact that there was no real, or even incipient, civil society in either Russia or Chechnya, no functioning democratic institutions headed by responsible, properly elected leaders who might have acted to avert war.

The fighting between Russia and its rebellious province broke out in earnest in December 1994 after Yeltsin signed a secret decree calling for the use of "all means available" to establish "legal order" in Chechnya. The quick-fix operation was supposed to have been over by mid-December, but when Russian forces moved into the area, they encountered determined resistance and weren't able to reach Grozny until late December. After relentless bombarding of the capital and other towns and villages, the Russian infantry moved into Grozny on December 31, 1994. That attack marked the real beginning of the first Chechen war.

The conflict dragged on for twenty-one months. There were small victories on both sides, but at enormous cost in the destruction of property and human life. There had also been two major hostage-taking incidents carried off by the Chechens. The most notorious one, which came close to ending the war, took place in June 1995 in the Russian city of Budennovsk, about one hundred and twenty kilo-metres north of Grozny. Yeltsin was away at a G-7 summit in Halifax, Nova Scotia, when it happened, leaving the Russian prime minister, Viktor Chernomyrdin, to deal with the crisis and negotiate an end to the standoff. Out of those talks came a truce that gave the Chechens a few months of respite before full-scale hostilities resumed that December.

In April 1996, the Chechen president, Dudayev, was killed by a Russian rocket that had homed in on his satellite phone. It was one of the few clear-cut Russian successes in the war, but what finally brought the Russians to settle was a counterattack by the Chechens the follow-ing August in which they managed to retake Grozny, once again at great cost to the city and its inhabitants, but reinforcing the myth of Chechen invincibility. On August 12, 1996, General Alexander Lebed, who was head of the Russian National Security Council and an oppo-nent of the war, went to the border town of Khasavyurt in Dagestan to meet with the new Chechen president, General Aslan Maskhadov. Together they agreed on a withdrawal of Russian troops from Chechnya, pending a resumption of talks on the territory's status in 2001. Maskhadov would continue as Chechen president.

The first Chechen war had set new benchmarks for brutality in the annals of post-Stalinist Russia. Grozny was mercilessly bombarded by Russian planes and artillery and set upon by ground troops. Large parts of what had once been a beautiful city, the centre of an oil industry, with shops, cafés, schools, hospitals, a university, quiet squares, and leafy residential districts, were reduced to ruin and rubble. The destruction of Grozny had been a pyrrhic victory for the Russians that left the inhabitants, many of whom were ethnic Russians, impoverished, homeless, and often destitute, and it destroyed much of what was left of the Chechen economy.

But what happened in Grozny was only the most spectacular part of the war. Elsewhere, away from the television cameras and the reporters, villages were pulverized, and thousands of civilians—men, women, and children—were shot, bombed, strafed from helicopters, gunned down at checkpoints, kidnapped, and tortured to death. Thousands more vanished without a trace. The death toll among Chechens was estimated to be close to 5 percent of the population. And thousands of Russians died as well. Memorial, a Russian organization that, among other things, monitors human rights violations in Russia, estimated that by the August 1996 truce, well over four thousand Russian servicemen had been killed, over seven hundred were missing or being held prisoner, and about the same number had deserted or gone missing.

The human rights abuses committed by both sides fill long reports painstakingly assembled by groups such as Memorial and Human Rights Watch, in the US. According to Memorial reports, the twenty-one-month conflict "in terms of the amount of violations of human rights, of the number of victims, and of [its] unusual brutality . . . exceeded anything seen in Russia since the end of the mass repression in the 1950s."

Unfortunately, rather than enjoying a respite from war in the late 1990s, Chechnya under the new leadership of President Aslan

Maskhadov disintegrated further into anarchy. Kidnapping became a lucrative way of life for many Chechen bandits and self-styled freedom fighters. As well, the ideas of Islamic fundamentalism were beginning to take hold. They were probably brought to the region by Arabs who had fought against the Russians in Afghanistan in the 1980s and were attracted to the idea of continuing that struggle in Chechnya. In the desperate suffering and poverty of Chechnya, Wahhabism, a fundamentalist Islamist movement that had its origins in Saudi Arabia, predictably began to find adherents among the young and the disaffected, including, it seems, Movsar Barayev and his gang, and the eighteen young women suicide bombers who were his accomplices.

The second Chechen war was launched by Vladimir Putin in 1999. The hostilities were triggered by two things. The first was an incursion into Dagestan in August 1999 by an international band of fighters led by the Chechen commander Shamil Basayev, the man who had carried off the hostage-taking at Budennovsk, and by an accomplice from the Middle East known as Al Katthab, a shadowy Che Guevara–like figure with possible connections to Osama bin Laden. It was largely his presence that lent credibility to Russian charges that Chechen terrorism was now internationally inspired and coordinated. The second trigger was a series of apartment bombings in and around Moscow in which over three hundred innocent people died. The Russian authorities immediately blamed it on the Chechens, although there is well-founded speculation that the bombings may have been carried out by the Russian security forces to create a *cause de guerre* shocking enough to justify renewed attacks on Chechnya.

The second Chechen war surpassed the first in sheer savagery, so much so that Memorial investigators likened the brutality of the conflict to a malignant virus infecting the whole of Russian society.

Ironically, while there was strong and growing opposition inside Russia to the first war, the second war generated anti-Chechen sentiments among the Russian public, and, apart from a tiny anti-war movement, almost no public opposition. One reason was that the second war, unlike the first, went largely unreported in the Russian media. This was partly because the Russian government was placing increasingly strict controls on the media by this time and partly because Chechnya had become so dangerous that few journalists would venture there. What scant official coverage there was came mostly from sources controlled by the Russian military.

Despite the clampdown on information, some of the horrifying details of this second conflict filtered through to the media and the world press, thanks mainly to the efforts of courageous journalists such as Russian reporter Anna Politkovskaya, Czech war correspondent Petra Procházková, and the Franco-Russian writer Anna Badkhen. From them, we know something of the terrible plight of ordinary Russians and Chechens living there, and about the course of the conflict. The war had been marked by "disappearances"—people rounded up in the middle of the night during the *zachistki,* the "mopping-up" operations, or arrested at a *blokpost* and never seen again—and by torture, rape, kidnapping, indiscriminate raids, mass executions, and wholesale destruction. Again, there were many deaths on both sides.

But at least two other factors made this second war stand out and a political solution even more unlikely. One was the deep involvement of criminal gangs, beholden to no one but themselves; the other was the introduction of Islamic fundamentalism into the already volatile mix of nationalism and crime.

And perhaps there was one more factor: as in the Middle East, the second Chechen war led to a rash of suicide bombings, mainly committed by desperate Chechen women. The first of these was a young woman named Khava Barayeva. In June 2000, she and a female accomplice drove a truck into a Russian Special Forces barracks in Alkhan Kala, killing themselves and twenty-seven soldiers. Barayeva's last known words were "I know what I am doing. Paradise has a price, and I hope this will be the price for Paradise."

Khava Barayeva was the sister of the Chechen terrorist Arbi Barayev, and she was Movsar Barayev's aunt. She was the precursor to the eighteen women who were now inside the House of Culture in Moscow, ready, like her, to blow themselves up.

8

THE HOUSE OF CULTURE

Wednesday, October 23   11:00 P.M.

We'd been captives for only a little more than two hours when Movsar entered the hall and stood in the aisle, facing the front, and addressed the audience. He reminded me of a politician trying to win votes, not of a terrorist issuing an ultimatum. He held his Kalashnikov in his left hand and gestured dramatically with his right as he spoke: "Get out your mobile phones. Call your friends and relatives. Tell them we are holding you hostage at the House of Culture," he said. "Tell them you are hostages of the Islamic Brigade of the Chechen army. Our demands are simple, and we are prepared to die for them. We want the Russian troops to withdraw from Chechnya. We want an end to the war. Tell them that if the Russians attack the building, you will all be blown up. Tell them that for every one of us they kill, we will kill ten of you." He paused, then added, "Tell them to remember

51

that we want to die more than you want to live." This last statement came almost an afterthought, but we'd heard it before. It was clearly a slogan the terrorists had been instructed to repeat as often as possible.

It was the first time we had heard the terrorists' demands stated in full, and there was absolute silence as the meaning of his words sank in. Everyone must have known that their demands would be impossible to fulfill. In the first place, Russian president Putin was known to be a hard-liner where Chechnya was concerned and was therefore unlikely to negotiate with the terrorists, let alone concede anything to them, not even when the lives of hundreds of his citizens were at stake. Beyond that, the demands themselves were completely unrealistic. How many Russian troops were in Chechnya? I didn't know. But certainly there were more of them than could be moved out at short notice.

And how much time did we have? Movsar had mentioned no deadline. How long could we go without eating or drinking? The only food and drink in the theatre were the snacks sold at the concession booths. There was nowhere to sleep, only the theatre seats, which were cramped and uncomfortable. How would we wash, or go to the bathroom, when, as far as I knew, the public washrooms were accessible only through the front lobby, in full view of the forces that had almost certainly gathered outside? How long were the terrorists prepared to hold eight hundred people hostage, in the middle of a hostile city, surrounded, we could well imagine, by platoons of soldiers, police officers, firefighters, reporters, television crews with their cameras, all desperate for a resolution? Who would crack first, the hostages, the terrorists, or the Russian forces? One thing was sure: Movsar's announcement had set the clock ticking.

But why were the terrorists asking us to make phone calls? The most obvious reason was that they were afraid the Russians, with their ability to control the media and their passion for secrecy, would drop a curtain of silence around the hostage-taking and no word of it, or of their cause, would get out. Hostage-taking doesn't work unless the public knows about it, and unless someone stands to be publicly humiliated. The terrorists must have thought that if several hundred sets of relatives started demanding a peaceful settlement, Putin would be under extreme pressure to negotiate, or at least to go through the motions. As well, they must have known that the theatre would be surrounded, and they hadn't yet finished planting all their explosives and booby traps. They weren't ready for the attack they knew must come. No doubt the terrorists thought that heartfelt appeals by the hostages themselves might stay the Russian government's hand, at least until they were ready to fight back. Getting us to call out was a way of buying more time.

Still, it was odd. Why hadn't they come prepared with a list of media people and politicians to contact? Why were they leaving it up to us to pass their message on to the world, and in such a haphazard way? Were we in the hands of people whose only real skill was causing death and destruction?

In Moscow, almost everyone has a cellphone with pre-paid air time. So throughout the theatre, hostages pulled out their cellphones and started phoning families and friends.

The big question was whom to call, and what to tell them? With a limited amount of air and battery time, this choice became paramount. How could we make the best use of the opportunity? Would we use it to reassure loved ones? Or to pass on the terrorists' message?

One of the young dancers sitting in front of us asked Movsar if we should be calling the newspapers, and he said, "Why not?" She reached over and snatched the paper that the old man had been reading, riffled through it until she reached the page with the editorial phone numbers, thrust it toward the terrorist, and said, "Shall I call or will you?"

"You call," he replied. She did.

Some people tried to call the emergency services. But it was naïve of them, for as they found out, the police already knew about the situation.

I finally decided to call Todor, a Bulgarian friend of mine in Moscow. I knew I could trust him to think of something useful to do in tight situations. When he answered, his voice sounded sleepy, and I realized that he was already in bed. "Have you heard the news?" I asked.

"What news?" he said.

"Listen," I said, "this is not a joke, so pay attention. I went to the theatre tonight, to a performance of *Nord-Ost*. The whole audience has been taken hostage. Please try to call someone, but don't call my family just yet. They might let me go."

There was a silence at the other end while Todor absorbed this. Then he said, "So, wait a minute, are you saying they won't let you leave Russia?"

"Who?"

"The Russians. Didn't you just say that Bush has been taken hostage?"

"Todor, wake up!" I said. "This is serious. Look, I'm at the House of Culture on Dubrovka Street. Call the Bulgarian embassy. Let them know what's going on, and then come down here. Bring your cellphone. They might be letting us go."

I gave the phone to Irina, but we had a problem. If she called her family, she'd have to speak Russian, and if the Chechen women who were sitting just a few metres away heard her, we would be in trouble. Irina decided to call Katya, a colleague at the language school. Katya spoke English fluently. It took a long time to get through, probably because so many people were trying to call out at the same time from the same place. When Katya finally answered, Irina told her what was going on.

People all around us were making phone calls. Most of the young dancers called their parents. Some were crying, others were putting on a brave front, saying things like "Mom, I'm at *Nord-Ost* but it's going to be okay." A lot of people asked their families to call the officials, the mayor of Moscow, or the police, but those authorities had long since been alerted. The main message was that the terrorists had booby-trapped the theatre, that it was set to blow up at the first sign of an attack by the police or the army, but that we were in no immediate danger. It was strange to hear people actually saying this. The danger felt all too immediate to me.

The act of calling out and talking to people on the outside seemed to have a calming effect on the hostages. We felt that we were doing something that might affect the course of events. We were buying time. We were beginning to realize that in this strange game we'd been caught in, we were of more use to the terrorists alive than dead.

At midnight, one of the Chechen women turned on the radio to see if the telephone calls we had made had been able to break though the silence that seemed to have descended over the theatre. When the news came on, she turned the volume up so that as many people as possible could hear it. What we heard was unsettling. One report said that the theatre had been captured not by Chechen rebels, or guerril-las, or freedom fighters, but by a violent gang of desperate criminals who were notorious for the indiscriminate killing of people, of Russians especially, and for taking hostages and holding them for ransom. They named Movsar Barayev as the head of this gang, which, the report said, was one of the most violent and bloody in Chechnya. To make matters worse, another report said that the theatre was already surrounded by the Special Forces, and that snipers from the dreaded Alpha Squad, the Russian army's crack rapid intervention team, had taken up positions outside. Clearly, the government was preparing to storm the building.

The news made me uneasy, but Irina was terrified. "I know the games they play here," she whispered. "These news reports are just a set-up. They don't give a damn about us, only about how they are going to explain the situation later on. I can already hear the news reports after the storming: 'Hundreds of innocent hostages have been killed but we have done our best,' the authorities will say. 'The criminal gang of terrorists was not interested in negotiations.'"

What if she was right? It was the first time I allowed myself to even consider the thought that we might die.

It would not be the last.

9

BUDENNOVSK

June 1995

The reason why the Russian hostages in the House of Culture on Dubrovka Street were worried about what the Russian authorities might do could be summed up in a single word: Budennovsk.

Budennovsk is a city of about one hundred thousand in the Stavropol region of Russia, not far from the Chechen border. On June 14, 1995—six months after hostilities in the first Chechen war had broken out in earnest, and at a time when the war was not going well for the Chechens—Shamil Basayev, the most experienced Chechen military field commander, took a group of about one hundred and fifty Chechen fighters and set out to carry the war from Chechnya into the heartland of Russia. The soldiers, dressed in Russian military uniforms, travelled in a convoy of two trucks and an escort car that had been repainted to resemble, to the casual eye, a Russian police vehicle. They made their way north, perhaps using their knowledge of the local terrain and the back roads to avoid the numerous *blokposti* or, if that were not possible, bribing their way through. Their cover story was that they were transporting coffins containing the bodies of Russian soldiers killed in the war back to Russia. Given the casualty rates, their story was entirely believable.

It was said that Basayev's ultimate destination was Moscow. Certainly the hope was that a bold and embarrassing "invasion" of the Russian capital would force the federal government to the negotiating table and bring the war to an end.

Although only thirty years old at the time, Shamil Basayev was already famous for his daring and unconventional military strategies, and his willingness to resort to bold acts of terror to achieve strategic ends. In 1991, when Jokhar Dudayev proclaimed Chechen independence, the Russian president, Boris Yeltsin, responded by declaring a state of emergency. Leading a small group of seven armed men, Basayev hijacked a passenger plane in Mineralnye Vody, just inside the Russian border, and forced it to fly to Ankara, Turkey, where he demanded to make a public statement insisting that the Russian government lift the state of emergency against Chechnya. The Turkish authorities refused, and the plane returned to Chechnya. This time, no one was killed or injured.

Over the next few years, Basayev fought in a number of local independence wars in the Caucasus region and then went on to train in guerrilla warfare tactics with the mujahedeen fighters in Afghanistan and Pakistan, where, according to some sources, he met Osama bin Laden. He returned to Chechnya in 1994.

The Russians invaded Chechnya in December 1994, but they made little headway until the following June, when they launched a massive military offensive, pushing the Chechens back until they held only a small piece of territory in the mountains. Yeltsin got ready to tell the upcoming G-7 conference in Halifax that the Chechen conflict would soon be over and that Russia would at last be a stable country, a good place in which to invest.

On June 14, Basayev's convoy of soldiers reached the outskirts of Budennovsk, where it was stopped by local police at a checkpoint and forced to go to police headquarters in the city centre. When they arrived, the Chechen fighters leaped out of the trucks, shot and killed several police officers, and occupied the headquarters. But because some of the Chechens had been seriously wounded in the skirmish, Basayev decided to take over the local hospital. The Chechens stormed the building and held anywhere from twelve hundred to two thousand terrified people—patients, staff, and visitors—hostage. They sealed off all the exits and announced their conditions for releasing the hostages: an end to the war in Chechnya, the withdrawal of Russian forces, and a settlement to be negotiated with Dudayev over the future of Chechnya as an independent country.

The Russians rushed an array of troops to the scene—the local militia, soldiers from a nearby helicopter base, units from the Alpha Squad Special Forces, and interior ministry troops—and began immediately laying plans to storm the hospital. Basayev threatened to kill the hostages if the Russians attacked, then positioned some of them in the windows as human shields. The Russian media arrived and started broadcasting live from the scene, turning the hostage-taking into a minute-by-minute drama followed in Russian households all the way from Kaliningrad to Vladivostok.

Two days later, on June 16, Yeltsin arrived in Halifax to take part in the G-7 conference, while back home, the Russian parliament debated possible impeachment procedures against him. Early the next morning, a Saturday, the Russian forces stormed the hospital but were

driven back by the Chechens. Basayev, hoping to demonstrate good-
will, released about one hundred and fifty hostages, mostly children
and pregnant women. The Russian forces regrouped and, in the early
afternoon, stormed the hospital again. Once more the Chechens beat
back their attackers.

When the shooting had stopped, over a hundred hostages lay dead,
all of them caught in the crossfire. There were Chechen and Russian
military casualties as well, and the politicians in Moscow fell over
themselves denying that they had given the orders to attack. But the
damage had been done. The *Moscow News,* perhaps echoing the public
mood, wrote: "June 17 will go down in the annals of the struggle
against terrorism as a day of folly, unprofessionalism [on the part] of
the military and the complete idiocy of their superiors."

It was a human and a public relations disaster, and rather than
risking another bloodbath, the Russian prime minister, Viktor
Chernomyrdin, decided to negotiate directly with Basayev. Incredibly,
the negotiations, which took place by phone, were broadcast live on
television, allowing everyone in the country to witness the Russian
government's humiliation as the prime minister pleaded with the
Chechens to stand down. In the end, Chernomyrdin agreed to a cease-
fire and peace talks, and to safe passage back to Chechnya for the
hostage-takers. It was a victory for terrorist tactics, and probably
marked the beginning of the end of Yeltsin's career.

While the safe passage was being arranged, many volunteers from
Moscow—members of parliament, members of human rights
groups—came to Budennovsk to offer themselves as substitute
hostages. One of these, Oleg Orlov, a leading member of the Moscow-
based human rights organization Memorial, was shocked by what he
found inside the hospital. Outside in the streets, Russian anger against
the Chechens was so acute that people were prepared, he said, "to tear
any Chechen they saw to pieces." But inside the hospital, he found the

hostages in the grip of an "enormously strong Stockholm Syndrome," the phenomenon in which hostages begin to sympathize and even identify with their captors. This was after the bungled storming by the Russian Special Forces, but it was also after they had seen the Chechens shoot ten hostages in cold blood, most of them young air cadets from a nearby military academy. The Chechens had also killed a man who had contrived to get into the hospital because his wife was a doctor there; the terrorists took him for a police agent and shot him.

Yet despite having witnessed these ruthless acts, Orlov said, some of the hostages, even out of earshot of the terrorists, insisted they had not been mistreated, and said they didn't consider the Chechens terrorists but legitimate "fighters." When they were about to be released, some of the hostages actually bade their captors teary farewells.

In the end, the surviving hostages were released, the hostage-takers boarded the six buses provided, each with his own personal human shield—a volunteer hostage—who sat in the window seat. Then they were all driven back to Chechnya, where the hostages were released, as promised. The Russians also provided a refrigerated truck so the Chechens could carry home their dead.

In the aftermath of this hostage-taking, Yeltsin, embarrassed internationally by the spectacular display of lethal incompetence by his own security forces, fired some key ministers and regional leaders. The temporary agreement negotiated with Chernomyrdin quickly broke down, and it wasn't until Grozny was retaken in August by Chechen forces led by Basayev that a truce was finally signed and hostilities, at least on a large, official scale, ceased.

The death of innocent civilians at Budennovsk left a bitter taste in the mouths of ordinary Russians. They saw it as proof that their own government was indifferent to their lives, and it strengthened a legacy of deep mistrust that still exists today.

10

THE HOUSE OF CULTURE

Thursday, October 24   1:00 A.M.

It was past midnight now and the theatre was quiet. Those whose cellphones were still working spoke with relatives or friends, confessing their fears, or reassuring them that everything was going to be all right. I thought of my family. I was still hoping that we would be released before they found out where I was. The thought of their anguish was harder for me to bear than the dangers we faced in the theatre.

Now that the explosives were in place, the authorities had lost an important advantage. The Special Forces would have to come up with ways to move in quickly enough to stop the terrorists from executing their deadly plan. But how could they do that without unleashing sudden and tremendous firepower and perhaps killing many of us in the process? There was an inherent flaw in the terrorists' strategy: to detonate all the bombs at once would not only require superhuman coordination, but if one of the suicide bombers blew herself up prematurely, she could kill some of her colleagues before they too had the chance to blow themselves up. Then again, if they were using self-detonating explosives, a single blast would set in motion a chain reaction of powerful explosions that could bring the theatre down on our heads.

It was about this time that the terrorists pulled together the sliding panels that had served as a curtain so that we could no longer see the stage. From now on, everything that took place on the stage, except for the metre or so of apron in front of the screens, was hidden from our sight. The male terrorists would come and go from behind the screen, where I thought they must have been sleeping or praying, or perhaps holding councils of war. They ran a wire across the apron of the stage connected to a bell that had been part of the play's set. If anyone tripped on the wire, the bell would ring—a simple alarm system that seemed almost laughable in this hi-tech setting. Then they took three of the chairs that were set at the end of each row and along the back of the theatre to seat an overflow audience, brought them onto the stage, placed them at roughly equal distance from each other, and taped packs of explosives to the backrests. Again, they connected the explosives with wires and attached a single detonator, which they gave to the woman who sat on the left side of the stage. With this, their preparations appeared to be at an end.

After pulling the sliding panels closed, they hung a black banner above the stage, and then suspended one in the balcony. Each displayed angular, white Arabic script. Someone in the audience asked what the words meant, and one of the terrorists translated it for us: "'There is no God but Allah and Mohammed is His prophet.'" He paused, then added: "'Victory or death.'" He paused again, and then corrected himself: "I mean, 'Victory or Paradise.'"

Again, I was reminded how precarious our situation was. For secular Chechen bandits, for hard-core separatist guerrillas, for Chechen nationalists and freedom fighters, hostages were a commodity, bargaining chips to be dealt away in exchange for money or weapons or tactical advantages. With such people, it might have been possible to make a deal of some kind. And the faint hope that such a deal could be negotiated was part of what had made me feel not entirely pessimistic about our situation. But what kind of deal could be made with suicidal fundamentalists? Was this hostage-taking really about ending the war in Chechnya? Or was something else at stake, something bigger than that, something in which we would be far less than bargaining chips and more like pawns in a chess game, of no value to either side except as sacrifices?

11

THE HOUSE OF CULTURE

Thursday, October 24   2:00 A.M.

Sometime after midnight, we heard more shooting and the sound of shattering glass. It sounded like an exchange of fire, and it was so loud that I thought it might even have been a stun grenade and that the forces had begun storming the theatre. Once more, we crouched under the seats—a tight fit, since the rows were so close together. A few minutes later, one of the terrorists came running in with blood gushing from his hand and asked if there was a doctor in the theatre. It would have been almost farcical if it hadn't been so dangerous: if he had been shot by someone from the outside, he might want to start shooting hostages in retaliation.

A woman sitting a few rows ahead of us stood up and announced that she was a doctor. She was about forty, with light brown hair and glasses, casually dressed in a sweater and trousers. She left her seat and went over to the man to look at his arm. Her manner was calm and self-assured, and from their conversation, I understood that he had cut himself seriously on broken glass. The woman—her name was Dr. Maria Shkolnikova and she was a well-known pediatrician—said that she needed a first-aid kit right away. A man with long hair and a loose tie, whom the terrorists had herded in from the lobby and shoved roughly into a seat, said there was a kit in one of the offices at the front of the building. The terrorists were reluctant to believe him, but Dr. Shkolnikova told them that if she couldn't stop the bleeding and treat the wound properly, it might become infected. Reluctantly, the terrorists let the man go for the first-aid kit, escorting him as far as the bottom of the stairs, leaving him to go to the office on his own. A couple of minutes later he returned with the kit and a bottle of water. Dr. Shkolnikova handed the wounded man the water and commanded him—she was becoming more confident by the minute—to wash the wound. Then she put some antiseptic on it and bandaged it expertly. It was all she could do at the moment, she said, but he'd need stitches as soon as possible.

Now that she had made contact with the terrorists, Dr. Shkolnikova took advantage of it. She told them she was at the theatre with her son and husband, and that her husband taught in Germany and had good connections there. Her husband told Movsar that he could contact the German media and help the terrorists get their message out. They agreed to release him, with a warning that if he didn't do what he'd promised, they still had his wife and son. They didn't say it in so many words, but the message was clear: unless he cooperated, he might never see his family alive again.

After the terrorists released her husband, Dr. Shkolnikova agreed to speak to the Russian media. Using someone's cellphone, she phoned radio stations, relaying to them what the terrorists told her to say— that more than four thousand children have been killed in the hostilities in Chechnya, that some of the women here (meaning the suicide bombers) had left their own children at home and come all the way to Moscow to carry out this act, that they believed everyone in the theatre was complicit in the war in Chechnya, and that the hostage-takers were ready for anything. The person on the other end of the phone must have asked to talk to one of the terrorists, but when Shkolnikova asked one if he'd like to say a few words, he said, "No, you do the talking."

Shkolnikova went on to plead as forcefully as she could that the authorities call off any plans they might have for storming the theatre. I remember vividly something she said: "Stop walking on our heads. They're treating us well; it's you who are killing us."

What did she mean by "walking on our heads?" Then I remembered hearing the beating of a helicopter outside. Could that have been used to hide the sounds of the Special Forces on the roof, trying to find a way into the theatre? The terrorists must have heard something too, because I had seen one of them, with a powerful flashlight taped to the barrel of his Kalashnikov, pointing at the ceiling and talking to the producer of *Nord-Ost,* Georgi Vasilyev. Vasilyev told me later that Movsar had wanted to rake the ceiling with machine-gun fire but that he persuaded him not to, telling him it was a specially constructed ceiling that might come crashing down.

With the sound of more shooting outside, we cowered under our seats just as Movsar strode into the hall and announced sarcastically that he'd killed a police officer who'd had too much to drink and come too close to the building. Then Yassir rushed into the hall and fired his gun into the air. People panicked, and I could hear several of them frantically calling on their cellphones and talking as though they thought the end was near. The girl next to me asked me what was going on, and I replied, with more bravado than I felt, "Nothing. I think they're just trying to frighten us." I turned to Irina, and she gave me a weak smile, as if to say, If that's what they're trying to do, it's working.

I was forcing myself to believe that this was true. I knew that if I gave in to fear or panic or despair, I wouldn't be of any use to anyone, least of all to myself. I understood that the terrorists had to keep us, and themselves, on edge. This display of rushing around and firing off their guns was indeed partly to frighten us, but it was also meant to keep themselves pumped and ready for anything. The lack of response from the government or from anyone who might talk to them was making them edgy. If the terrorists were nervous and trigger-happy, it was probably also because they sensed that the Special Forces were already inside the theatre, somewhere, waiting. When the Russians finally did decide to attack, there would be no advance warning.

12

OUTSIDE THE HOUSE OF CULTURE

Wednesday, October 23

When the news of the hostage-taking first reached the authorities, squads of police officers and members of the Special Forces rushed to the theatre and, using armoured personnel carriers, police cars, fire engines, and commandeered buses, sealed off the access routes and neighbouring streets. A wet snow was still coming down and the immediate area was utterly deserted, except for the cars in the parking lot belonging to those in the audience who were now being held hostage inside. The lobby was completely dark; the terrorists had obviously turned off the lights. There were three other vehicles in the lot: two SUVs—a Ford and a Chevrolet—and a Russian-made minivan. They had been driven by the terrorists, who must have rushed the theatre the moment they arrived, because the vehicle doors were still open, and their lights had been left on. Clearly, they had no intention of using them as getaway cars.

Several levels of security were at the scene. The officers of the Federal Security Service (FSB), successor to the KGB, were in charge of the area, but there were also personnel from the City Division for Combating Organized Crime and troops belonging to the army and the Ministry of the Interior. The power to the surrounding streets was cut, but not to the theatre itself. The areas in front of the theatre and around it were dark, making it hard for the terrorists to see out the windows. Television crews arrived, along with radio and print journalists and gathering crowds of onlookers. The streets within half a kilometre on all sides of the theatre were blocked so that no unauthorized vehicles or persons could come near it.

The Russians set up a command post in a building not far from the theatre. They established telephone and computer links and ordered the cellphone companies to start monitoring cellphone traffic from inside the building. They obtained detailed plans and drawings of the theatre and officers made sure that no one else had access to them. The operation was given a code name—"Thunderstorm," an ominous reference to the ultimate goal, which was to storm the building and bring the hostage-taking to an end.

The elite division of the Special Forces—the Alpha Squad— arrived on the scene fifteen minutes after receiving the alert, and it wasted no time in getting some of its members inside the theatre complex. One group entered the nightclub for gay patrons, which had separate premises in the northeastern corner of the building. This placed them close to the backstage area of the theatre, but with no direct access to it. Snipers swiftly spread out around the building, positioning themselves either on the ground, behind any available shelter, such as cars in the parking lot, or on the rooftops of the surrounding apartment buildings, most of which were no more than six or seven storeys but which nevertheless provided a commanding view of the theatre complex.

Around midnight on Wednesday, a reporter for the *Moscow Times,* an English-language newspaper, saw a dozen armed men in riot gear run up to the theatre. According to Ekho Moskvy, a local radio station that carried live coverage throughout the hostage-taking, the men actually entered the theatre but then retreated, possibly under fire from inside. There were also reports of a firefight directly in front of the theatre.

Meanwhile, some of the actors and theatre employees who weren't in the auditorium or lobbies when the hostage-taking began had managed to escape. People working backstage in the costume department heard shooting, saw on the backstage television monitors what was happening, and ran to the third floor, where they locked themselves in a room and called the police. When the Special Forces arrived, they signalled them using the light from their cellphone displays, then fashioned a crude rope from curtains and slid to the ground. Members of the Special Forces who had already entered the building, possibly through the stage door at the back, managed to lead others to safety. Still others on the outside brought ladders to help people get out of the building.

Maria Shyorstova, the actor who played the mature Katya, the romantic lead in *Nord-Ost,* was in the wings with some of the other actors when the terrorists burst in. They were able to slip into a dressing room, lock themselves in, and then, sometime later, escape through a window.

There is no agreement on how many people inside the theatre managed to escape or how many, like the children and a handful of adult hostages, were released in the first twelve hours. Estimates range anywhere from fifty to one hundred.

Some Special Forces officers managed to get onto the roof, but once there they could find no access to the building. Other officers discovered a way into the basement, which the terrorists never fully controlled; the officers installed listening devices wherever they could to monitor movements and conversations inside the theatre. Over the next two days, using both electronic probes and any visual contact they were able to maintain, they tracked the whereabouts of most of the terrorists, making sure that as far as possible they could quickly identify them once they went in. They also knew approximately where the terrorists had placed the bombs and the booby traps, and, in the early hours of the hostage-taking, they could watch them taking the hostages to the washrooms in the basement, as the route led, for a very short distance, through the front lobby. They claim to have had an agent in the audience, someone who had gone to the theatre on his night off and who was surreptitiously sending information to them using the short messaging system on his cellphone.

The Alpha Squad had planned to storm the theatre as soon as it was in position, but the officers—or someone higher up—quickly realized that without accurate intelligence from inside the theatre and a carefully devised and rehearsed plan of attack, they ran the risk of botching the rescue effort, as they had done in Budennovsk. It was one thing for matters to go awry in an obscure town in the far reaches of Russia, but this was Moscow, the theatre was ringed with media satellite dishes, and reporters from major Western newspapers were asking all kinds of questions and filing stories, sometimes several times a day. Despite the fact that the story of the Beltway sniper was dominating headlines in the US, the story from Moscow was beginning to attract worldwide attention. The Russian politicians who were meeting to discuss the situation must have known this, and known that they could ill afford another highly public debacle. Putin was in the international spotlight, and his reputation depended on a successful outcome.

Once the hostages started phoning out on their cellphones, the security team was able to determine their cellphone numbers, then phone into the theatre and talk directly to the hostages. They would ask the hostages to put the terrorists on the phone so they could talk to them, but the terrorists would refuse.

When the extent of the threat became clear, steps were taken to protect the residents in the neighbourhood. Apartment buildings within range of the theatre were evacuated, and when daybreak came, classes in all nearby schools were cancelled. Farther from the site, the police increased the security at many public buildings, at train and bus terminals, and at the Moscow international airport.

Politicians also began appearing at the scene. The mayor of Moscow, Yuri Luzhkov, showed up, along with Prosecutor General Vladimir Ustinov. There was a spokesman from the Kremlin, and many members of the Duma—the Russian parliament—came as well. It was about this time, too, that Aslanbek Aslakhanov, the lone Chechen deputy in the Duma, tried to meet with Movsar Barayev. Movsar refused. Mostly, though, throughout that long, wet night and into the next day, the authorities were working hard to assess what was going on inside the theatre, using what information they could get from the monitored phone calls, from direct observation, and from debriefing the rattled but relieved hostages who had escaped or had been released.

Since giving in to the terrorists' demands was out of the question, those at the centre of Operation Thunderstorm would have to play for time while coming up with ways to get as many hostages out as possible. By morning, President Putin had postponed a meeting in Berlin with the German chancellor, Gerhard Schroeder, and a weekend trip to an APEC forum in Mexico for a summit with US president George W. Bush. Instead, he convened a meeting with his staff and the prime minister, Mikhail Kasyanov. Soon afterward, Kasyanov's spokesman outlined the Kremlin's strategy on a local radio station, which the terrorists must have been monitoring on their own transistor radios. He summed up the government's position this way:

it is important to negotiate with the gunmen, but we are not going to make any concessions.

It was an extraordinary act of indiscretion, one that in effect tipped the government's hand to the terrorists, and it was just one of many indications that despite the appearance of well-planned professionalism, the authorities were often acting at cross-purposes. Moreover, with hostages and terrorists alike phoning out on cellphones and the media milling about and broadcasting live from the scene, there was little way the authorities could exercise any control over what the terrorists inside knew, or did not know, about their intentions.

At one point, the Special Forces took matters into their own hands. Alpha Squad officers smashed a television camera belonging to one of the Russian networks while it was broadcasting a live transmission showing troop movements near the theatre. Such a broadcast was, of course, a serious breach of security. But the incident need never have happened had there been a clear policy on press access like the British D-Notice, which in the interests of public security obliges the media in certain clearly defined circumstances, such as a hostage-taking incident, to limit what it prints or broadcasts.

As it was, there were huge gaps and inconsistencies in how the Russian authorities conducted operations at the scene. And it was probably those gaps that allowed some people to slip through the cordon around the theatre—with tragic results.

13

THE HOUSE OF CULTURE

Thursday, October 24   1:00 A.M.

In the early-morning hours of Thursday, a young woman appeared at the back left-hand entrance to the auditorium, not far from where we were sitting. She burst through the door as though she'd been shoved from behind. For a few seconds, she just stood there, staring. She was in her early twenties, slim, of medium height, with blond hair and intense dark eyes. She was wearing a jacket, black jeans, and a sweater, and I remember that her nose was red, as if she'd just come in out of the cold.

What would she have seen? A scattered array of despondent people slumped in the narrow seats in various attitudes of fatigue and fear; no sound except for the creaking of the seats, the shuffling of feet, whispered conversations; she might have caught the slightly acrid smell of sweat. She would have seen, at regular intervals around the perimeter of the audience, sitting on chairs leaning against the wall or pacing back and forth, veiled young women, mostly about her own age, clutching pistols, with bombs strapped around their waists; on stage, a black banner in a foreign script, and two or three masked men in camouflage gear lounging on the floor.

I watched as she hesitated, then saw two terrorists come through the door behind her and push her down the aisle, where a group of Chechen men were standing by the lower exit, talking. At first the men were taken aback. Her attitude was so bold and forthright it was obvious she was not a hostage. She tried to walk past the men to the stage, but one of them stepped into her path and tried to push her back. Movsar, who was on the stage, jumped down and took charge. "How did you get in here?" he yelled.

"I've been coming here since I was a child," she retorted. "I went to music school here. I know this building." She spoke firmly, with no hint of fear in her voice, glaring at them as though she had a perfect right to be there: it was they, not she, who were the intruders. The terrorists were looking at each other, perplexed, wondering what to make of this person who had slipped unchallenged past the guards they had posted outside, past the booby traps, and waltzed in here, straight into the very heart of their operation. But what seemed to perplex them even more was that she showed no fear.

"Sit down and shut up," Movsar said. He took her by the shoulder and pushed her roughly into an empty seat, two rows ahead of us. But the instant he let go of her, she was on her feet again. "Who do you think you are?" she said, pushing Movsar away. "You should be ashamed of yourselves! Look how you've terrified everyone! It's a disgrace!" Then she turned to the audience and said, in a voice that made me wonder if she'd been drinking, "Is this the time to be scared? Look how many of you there are! Why are you sitting here like sheep? You have to do something!"

Movsar stared at her for a moment, as though he couldn't believe this was happening. Then he said: "Execute her!"

By this time, we were all on the edge of our seats, watching. Some people called out, "No, don't do it! Don't shoot!"

But Movsar pointed to the double exit doors near the stage. "Take her out and kill her!" he said.

The woman's response was surprising. "Okay," she said, "come on." She was taunting them, daring them to act. With her head held high, she turned toward the door. It was an astonishing display of bravado.

People in the audience began pleading. "Can't you see she's drunk?" someone shouted, and indeed, that seemed the best explanation.

One of the terrorists took her by her upper arm and thrust her against the doorway, but she turned one last time to face us. I could see her expression clearly—it was still defiant. He pushed her in the chest, forcing her to back into the hallway. Then, when she was out of our sight, he raised his Kalashnikov, cocked it slowly and deliberately, and fired several times. Some people in the audience screamed. He closed the door and walked away.

For a long time, it was utterly silent. Then Movsar said, addressing us in Russian, "She wasn't a hostage. She was from the Special Forces. They did the same thing in Budennovsk—they sent someone into the hospital pretending to be drunk, but he was a spy, sending information to the forces outside. So we shot him, like we shot her."

I simply couldn't believe it. Why would the Special Forces have tried to infiltrate someone so young and impetuous into a situation so volatile and potentially violent, or given her a mission as foolhardy as trying to provoke the hostages into rising up against their captors? Movsar's claim that she was a Special Forces operative seemed outlandish; I could scarcely even believe they'd really killed her.

Later, from accounts in the press, we found out a little more about the woman. Her name was Olga Romanova, and she was twenty-six years old. She had lived in a small flat in an older, five-storey apartment building not far from the theatre, where she looked after her mother and brother, both of whom suffered from some kind of handicap. She'd trained as a cook but at the time of the hostage-taking she was working in a boutique that sold French perfume. She had ambitions to be an actor and had taken music and acting lessons when she was a child in the very building where we were being held. When it was first built in the 1970s, it would have sponsored programs in theatre and music for neighbourhood children, as well as for the sons and daughters of the ball-bearing company employees.

According to her co-workers in the boutique, Olga was working late that night, but when she heard the news of the hostage-taking on the radio, she had been outraged and told her colleagues she was going to do something about it. She went home after work and sat with her mother at the kitchen table, talking about what she could do to help. Were they drinking as they talked? Perhaps—it's common enough in Russia. At one point, her mother recalled later, Olga got up and said, "Mom, I'm going over there. I'm going to persuade them to release the women and children." Her mother tried to stop her, but Olga was used to getting her own way. She left the flat and walked out into the icy night.

What happened next, no one knows. The television cameras trained on the empty square in front of the theatre that night caught the image of a young woman walking alone in the rain across the parking lot, brushing by the very vehicles the terrorists had used to get to the theatre. Somehow, she had managed to slip past the police lines. The camera shows her walking straight up to the glass doors of the theatre's main entrance. She tries each door in turn, but they are all locked. She then walks purposefully to her left, along a columned arcade on the north side of the theatre, where she disappears from view.

A short time later, she appeared in the doorway of the auditorium, a few steps from where we were sitting.

When I think of the look on her face and her behaviour, I think she must have been someone blessed, or perhaps cursed, with natural courage, the kind of person who in certain moments can be utterly fearless, willing to go into life-and-death situations without worrying about whether she will get out alive, seemingly driven by a kind of impulsive determination. The important thing is to make a stand, not whether that stand makes sense.

In retrospect, it's easy to say that she was foolish, that she never stood a chance. Her kind of courage could only enrage the terrorists because it is infectious. The last thing they wanted was an uprising of hundreds of people inspired by the irrepressible spirit of this young woman. So they invented an excuse. They said she was with the police—and then they shot her in cold blood.

Later I asked one of the actors, Oleg Golub, who was sitting near the exit where she was shot, if he had believed they had killed her. "I knew they had," he said. "I heard her cry out. I smelled the gunpowder. I wish I could have convinced myself that she was still alive, but she couldn't have survived."

It was Yuri, the man who ran the snack bar in the lobby, who confirmed it for us. Like me, Yuri hadn't believed that they'd really shot and killed her. A while later, he needed to relieve himself. The terrorists had apparently given little thought to sanitary arrangements and they were escorting people to the bathrooms as the need came up. With dozens of hostages ahead of him waiting to be taken to the bathroom, Yuri had become desperate. He asked one of the women terrorists if he could slip out and use the hallway and she agreed. So he walked through the door. Olga's twisted body was lying on the hallway floor, her head toward the window opposite the door, a dark pool of blood congealing on the marble flagstones.

For more than a day her body lay there untended before the terrorists allowed it to be removed. According to the forensic examination, she had been struck in the chest at point-blank range; her fingers were shattered and burned, as though she had held up her hands in a vain attempt to defend herself and ward off the bullets.

The murder of Olga Romanova was a turning point. We had all been given a taste of what these people were capable of. They would not hesitate to kill if it suited them, and they were willing to tell the most transparent lies to justify their actions.

Later I read that the night before she died, Olga had had a dream. She saw herself brushing her hair. In her dream her hair was long and very thick and hard to comb. Her mother said this meant that she had a long road ahead of her.

14

THE GYMNASIUM
MELNIKOVA STREET

Wednesday, October 23, 9:15 P.M., to Thursday, October 24, Early Morning

Many of those who showed up outside the theatre that night were relatives of the hostages. Raisa Albina's story is probably typical. At about 9:15 on Wednesday evening, Raisa and some of her family, including grandchildren, were sitting at home watching television when a news "crawl" appeared at the bottom of the screen announcing that terrorists had overrun the House of Culture on Dubrovka Street and were holding hundreds of people hostage. There were no more details. Raisa's son, Oleg Golub, was a member of the cast. He had been on stage, dressed as a young air cadet and leading the chorus in the dance routine, when the terrorists took over the auditorium, though of course Raisa didn't know that at the time. Raisa immediately swung into action. Within five minutes, she and her younger son were in a car speeding through the Moscow streets toward the theatre. As they roared onto Dubrovka Street, a broad avenue lined with drab apartment blocks, they were forced to a screeching halt by a police barricade.

Raisa is a formidable woman, statuesque and maternal, with a powerful and commanding presence. Screaming, "My son is in there!" and demanding to be allowed through, she lambasted the Russian police officers with merciless invective until they let her past the barrier. As she approached the theatre complex, she encountered what looked like a chaotic melee of reporters, soldiers, and police officers. She sought out other relatives of hostages who had managed to get through the barricades, all clamouring for more information about what had happened, all trying to find out how the authorities were planning to deal with the situation. No one could, or would, tell them anything.

The police soon decided to herd the rapidly swelling crowd of distraught relatives into a gymnasium in a school on Melnikova Street, not far from the theatre. Television screens were installed, and the families were encouraged by the police not to leave. They sat staring at the screens in a state of shock. With no information other than what they could gather from the television, they began to feel like hostages themselves.

More relatives arrived. Some called home to find that their children, their wives, their husbands, their mothers, their fathers had, in the meantime, called them from inside the theatre. The messages were disturbing and terrifyingly similar: stop the Russian forces from storming the building at all costs or we will all be dead. The second part of the message was also the same: I love you.

In the gymnasium Raisa met Viktor, whose teenaged daughter, Tatiana, had gone to the performance with two friends. Viktor's wallet was thick, stuffed with photographs of his family, which he would frequently bring out and show around. Raisa and Viktor also met Svetlana, a science teacher and school principal, whose twenty-year-old son, Dennis, had gone to the theatre with friends. They comforted Natasha, an actor whose husband had a role in *Nord-Ost* and was trapped inside the theatre.

The parents and other relatives who had been shunted into the gymnasium felt they had a right to know what was going on and to have a say in the matter. Out of desperation, Raisa, Viktor, Svetlana, and Natasha, together with some other relatives, decided to take action. They formed a steering committee and began to plan a coordinated initiative. They had no experience in organizing in this way, and no real strategy, so they began at the beginning, by drawing up a list of people they knew were inside, starting with their own loved ones. The best way to help them, they felt, was to think of ways to put pressure on the authorities, and to make their voices heard.

15

THE HOUSE OF CULTURE

Thursday, October 24   5:00 A.M.

Shortly after Olga's death, Movsar was hurrying down the aisle beside us when a woman of about seventy approached from the other side of the theatre. "Stop that man! I want to talk to him," she shouted.

Movsar turned to face her.

"My husband is extremely ill," the woman said. "He's just had a bypass and his heart's very weak. He was a little boy when he was taken to a concentration camp in Tadzhikistan, and he was there for years. He's suffered so much all his life, and now, if you don't let him go, I'm afraid he'll die." Tears were streaming down her cheeks.

"No," Movsar said. "Go back and sit down. I'm not letting him go."

"You have to!"

Movsar drew his pistol and pointed it at her. Everyone in the theatre was watching, horrified. "If you don't get back to your place right now," he said, "I'll shoot you."

"Shoot me if you must," she replied defiantly, her hands on her hips, "but I'm not moving until you let my husband go."

We watched tensely as Movsar eased back the safety catch of his pistol. "Do as he says!" people in the audience began shouting. "Don't upset him! Go back to your seat! Sit down!" But she held her ground until a man nearby stood up, took her by the arm, and gently led her back to her place while she rested her head on his shoulder and sobbed.

Movsar watched them go, his pistol raised, as though still wondering whether he should shoot. When they reached their seats, he turned his back on them and walked away. I took a deep breath, reached up to wipe the sweat from my face, and realized that the sweat was really tears running down my cheeks. I quickly brushed them away, hoping no one would notice. I couldn't let the terrorists know they could make men cry, but in this situation, I couldn't help myself. I realized that this woman had reminded me of my mother. I had always admired my mother's strength and spirit, and I could imagine her now, behaving as this woman had here. My mother had lived through some very hard times, especially after my father's death, but she was not one to give up or back down. Thinking about her gave me a new sense of determination.

At around five o'clock on Thursday morning, a group of terrorists appeared on the stage and announced that they would soon be dealing with the foreigners. They told us to get our papers ready for inspection, then vanished behind the screen. While we were waiting, Irina leaned over to me and whispered, "I have my driver's licence and bank card with me. If they search me, they'll know I'm not Canadian."

This was a serious problem. "Take them out of your wallet when they're not looking," I whispered. "We'll hide them somewhere."

"That's not a good idea," Irina replied. "If they find them, they'll know who I am just by looking at the picture."

I thought for a moment. "Give me the cards, but try to do it so they don't see us."

Irina opened the *Nord-Ost* program on her lap, put the incriminating cards inside it, and passed it to me. I slid one shoe off with the other foot, and then, bending down as if to put it on again, I took Irina's driver's licence—a piece of plastic about twice the size of a credit card—along with her bank card and slipped them inside my sock, then put the shoe back on.

The men re-emerged from behind the screen and Movsar told us to get our passports ready and line up to have them looked at. We all lined up in the middle aisle, moving slowly forward as they checked our papers one by one. Yassir, the man who had first looked at our passports, was among them. I was hoping we could talk to him, because he might remember us, and I wouldn't have to repeat the same story all over again. Another terrorist was a man they called Abu Bakar. I'd never seen him without his mask, but he was recognizable by the goatee visible through his mouth hole. Later I observed from his manner, and the way other terrorists would defer to him, that his authority among them was almost as high as Movsar's. His eyes were steely and unrelenting and I prayed he wouldn't be the one we had to deal with.

The line inched forward. As luck would have it, when we finally reached the front, it was Movsar who was free to deal with us. I noticed that the butt of his Kalashnikov had a row of notches carved into it. Faltering momentarily, I explained that I was a Bulgarian with landed immigrant status in Canada and that my wife—Irina—had given her passport to the police and therefore had no papers with her. But

Movsar was unmoved. "If she has no passport, we won't release her," he said. "Go away."

By this time Irina had the English routine down cold and she asked me, in English, what he had said, and I repeated it, also in English. Movsar watched our exchange closely and then asked, "What's going on?"

"She doesn't speak Russian," I said. "I was translating what you just said."

"What does she speak?" he said.

"Only English."

He hesitated a moment, and then said, "Okay, okay," and he waved us both away.

The foreigners were directed to sit at the front on the left side of the centre aisle. Irina and I ended up in the front row, in seat numbers three and four, just below the side apron of the stage where one of the women terrorists was sitting. There was very little room between our seats and the stage, and we felt hemmed in.

When all the foreigners had been checked and seated, Movsar came over and explained that they were going to let us go at dawn, but that first they wanted us to call our ambassadors and ask them to be present when we were released. The Russians, he said, were not to be trusted: in Budennovsk, the Russians had shot hostages through the windows in the hospital and then blamed their deaths on the Chechens. "We don't want you to be killed," Movsar said, "and we don't want the Russians to be able to say we kill foreigners."

Abu Bakar, who was sitting next to Movsar as though he were his deputy, said, in a low voice so that only those close to him could hear, "We know that this is not your war. We're at war with the Russians. They've killed our children and our women, and if necessary we will die here. But we have nothing against you."

Abu Bakar was dressed differently from the others—more like a

Russian soldier—and he spoke to us in almost unaccented Russian; in fact, he spoke the language so well I thought he might actually have been a Russian. He certainly didn't behave like the other terrorists. The Chechen men were mostly a wary bunch, seldom looking people in the eye. When they moved, they moved quickly and stealthily, hunched over with their guns down low, making little noise, and preferring not to remain for long in exposed positions, like men used to fighting in mountain forests. Movsar, I noticed, was very uneasy when speaking to the hostages as a group. Abu Bakar, on the contrary, seemed to enjoy striking poses, and he walked with a deliberately heavy step, as though he enjoyed the effect he made, the attention it brought to him. Now he was sitting on the stage, swinging his legs, and I could see that he was wearing a pair of expensive Ecco boots that were popular in Moscow at the time.

"We could release you right now," Abu Bakar said, "but it's still dark and we'd rather do it in daylight, to make sure the media see the transfer. That way, nothing happens to you. So we are going to release you at dawn."

16

THE HOUSE OF CULTURE

Thursday, October 24   6:00 A.M.

There were about sixty foreigners sitting in the front eight rows; about half the group, by my estimate, were Ukrainians. One of them, sitting directly to my right (Irina was on my left) was a terrified young woman who put her head on my arm, even though she didn't know me. I could feel her trembling, but when I tried to calm her down and tell her that everything was going to be okay, she became very chatty. She asked me how to say things in Bulgarian and told me odd details of her life. She told me she had children of her own, but that they were too young to take to the theatre. "I came with my nephew," she said. "He's Russian."

"How old is he?" I asked.

"Eleven," she said.

"That's a relief," I said. "They must have let him go."

"No," she said. "He's tall for his age. They wouldn't believe he was only eleven, so they wouldn't let him go."

I was surprised. "Where is he now, then?" I asked. "Why isn't he here with you?"

"Well," she said, "I told you, he's Russian. He has Russian papers. They'd never have let him go with me. He's over on the other side of the theatre."

"Are you just going to leave him here?"

"No," she said. "Actually, I was hoping you might not mind pretending that he's your son. Maybe they'd let him go then."

It was a preposterous suggestion, but I tried to let her down gently. "Does he speak English?"

"No," she said. "Why, is that important?"

"Yes, it is," I said. "We've already told them I'm Bulgarian, and my wife speaks only English, and two of the leaders have already heard our story. They're simply not going to believe us if we go back and say we have a son who can't speak to his mother."

She was practically crying now, and she asked me to approach an American hostage, Sandy Booker, who was sitting several rows behind us, to ask him if he'd be willing to try. She was so terrified she wasn't thinking straight.

"That won't work either," I said, "for the same reason. Nobody will believe you. But look, I'm sure everything is going to be all right." And I ran through a list of reasons why I thought none of us was going to die. "There are some good signs," I told her. "In the first place, the terrorists aren't drinking, so I don't think they're going to suddenly go berserk and start shooting us. In the second place, they're mostly quite polite, and some of the women seem kind and understanding. One of them even seemed apologetic. They know that we're not personally responsible for the war in Chechnya, and I don't think they really want to kill us. Look, we're more useful to them alive than dead, aren't we?"

My arguments seemed to calm her down, and she soon fell asleep. I could see that other hostages had dozed off too, some of them slumped in their seats, or resting their heads on their arms, leaning on the row ahead of them. Like me, Irina couldn't sleep, so she passed the time talking to the hostage on her left, a young Lithuanian man who spoke English well and seemed remarkably cheerful. I remembered having seen him in the line ahead of us. He was short and rather portly, and he had joked about his pot-belly with one of the terrorists, suggesting that he was pregnant and should be let go. His name was Aleksander Zeltzerman and though he was only twenty-nine, he was a school principal back in Vilnius. He was at the theatre with his mother and his sister, and when the terrorists checked their passports and discovered they were Jewish (all internal passports in the former Soviet empire—and I assume it's true of Lithuania as well—show the ethnicity of the bearer, as well as their nationality) they got very excited and seemed to think it was funny to have found Jews in their midst. They laughed and made a point of telling everyone about it.

Aleksander's mother was the executive director of a special school, and his sister, Kira, was a student in Moscow. Aleksander and his mother had come to Moscow for a two-day trip to see some theatre. His sister had insisted on coming to *Nord-Ost,* and they had planned to see another play the next day. Aleksander couldn't resist ribbing Kira about her "excellent" choice.

Kira had a Walkman and she was listening to the news and keeping us informed about what was going on outside the theatre, at least as much of it as was being allowed to be broadcast. What struck me as odd, though, was that the Zeltzermans weren't sitting together but, rather, kept as far apart as they could in the "foreigners' section." They didn't even try to communicate with each other much. When I asked him about it, he said, "I can't stand sitting near my mother. She's such an alarmist."

Aleksander seemed incredibly relaxed, almost unconcerned. He spent most of the time dozing or sleeping. His attitude could be summed up by the phrase, "Wake me when it's over." It was enviable, but when I asked him how he could remain so calm in this situation, he shrugged and said, "I'm a school principal. There's not much I haven't seen."

The occasions to laugh were rare, and when we did, it was a great relief. But there was also a streak of common sense in Aleksander's behaviour. There wasn't much he could do at that moment, and he felt it was better to conserve his energy than to waste it on pointless efforts that could only make matters worse. Things did get worse, of course, and when they did, Aleksander rose to the occasion. But for now, he rested and found humour where he could.

Another member of our group was Natalia Zhirova. She had Dutch citizenship but was originally from western Ukraine. She was visiting Moscow and had come to the theatre with her teenaged son, a fair-haired boy with intelligent eyes. Natalia was a pretty woman of about forty, wearing a dark suit with a white blouse. She looked like a confident Western businesswoman, but of all the people who were near us in the foreigners' section, she was the most visibly upset and seemed constantly on the verge of tears. Earlier, when we were sitting at the back of the theatre, she had buttonholed one of the terrorists, Yassir, and told him how she had lived in the Netherlands for many years, that her son had been born there, what her life was like, why she'd come to Moscow, how she happened to be in the theatre, and so on.

Yassir wasn't interested in her nervous chatter, but I noticed that kind of thing happening a lot. People would approach the terrorists and tell them details about their lives that the Chechens could barely have understood, let alone cared about. I found myself doing it, too. At one point, I tried to tell Yassir that Canada was one of the few countries in the world that took in Chechen refugees. I got only a

blank stare in return and felt foolish for having mentioned it. Was I
trying to impress him? Or was I merely trying to imprint myself on
his mind, so that if the awful time came to select ten or fifty or a
hundred of us for execution, he would remember me, connect me with
a place that had shown their refugees some mercy, and pass me over?
Whatever the reason, I, too, was babbling, and was probably more
upset than I knew. In such a state of mind, almost anything you say or
do seems better than nothing.

Though Natalia sometimes seemed on the edge of losing control,
her teenaged son remained remarkably cool, at least on the outside. He
behaved very maturely. Once she called the Dutch embassy on her
cellphone and became extremely upset, frantically pleading with them
to intervene, not to let the Russians storm the building, to do something, anything, to help them, to get them out. Her son was gentle
with her and tried to calm her down—and it was a relief when he
succeeded. Irina and I were impressed by his bravery.

A young man from England sat not far from us, flanked by his
parents. Peter Low was studying in Moscow and his mother and father
were visiting him. The three of them sat quietly and said little, shining
examples of the stiff upper lip, but they were obviously scared.

The American in our group, Sandy Booker, was from Oklahoma
City. He had come to the theatre with his fiancée, Svetlana, and her
daughter, to celebrate the fact that the Americans had just given them
visas to enter the US. I didn't speak to Sandy much because he was
sitting eight rows behind me, but his story was so unusual that it got
passed around among the hostages like gossip. Sandy was divorced, in
his late forties, and worked as an electrician for General Motors. He
was also fond of languages; recently, he'd been studying Russian and
learned it well enough to start up a correspondence with Svetlana, who
was from Kazakhstan, and whom he'd met on the Internet. On an
earlier visit, they'd hit it off and become engaged, and he'd come back

to take her home with him. After picking up her visa at the American embassy, they stopped at a kiosk in the subway and bought three tickets to *Nord-Ost,* much as Irina and I had done at the last minute. Here they were, two adults and a child on the threshold of a new life, and they were stuck in this awful situation. I felt an empathy with him, and when we did talk, he seemed to find some comfort in meeting someone from the same continent.

Sandy had been a volunteer rescue worker after the Oklahoma City bombing, in 1995. So this was his second brush with terrorism, only now he was right in the middle of it. He seemed stoical about it. His Russian wasn't good enough to follow everything that was being said, so he spent his time observing. I remember his remarking to me, "You know, these guys are just kids," meaning the terrorists. It was something I simply hadn't paid attention to—to me, they were grown men with lethal weapons and a deadly mission. That, and their masks, had made their age seem irrelevant. But Sandy was right: most of the terrorists were in their twenties, and one or two of them were probably still teenagers. Certainly, most of the women were very young.

Realizing this, though, didn't make me feel sorry for them; it only made me angrier. Of course, like everyone one else, I tried to be polite and reasonable when I spoke to them, but that was just common sense, an instinct for self-preservation. Provoking them was the last thing I wanted to do, and I began to wonder how much of the behaviours grouped together under the notorious Stockholm Syndrome could be explained very simply by the intuitive sense people have for behaving in ways they believe, rightly or wrongly, will save their skins. Perhaps all those apparently odd behaviours are just efforts to allay the anger you should rightly feel—as Olga did—toward the hostage-takers, anger that might drive you to do something foolish. Or perhaps they help you resist hopelessness and despair by giving you the illusion that you are doing something. I could see people around me just sitting by themselves, their heads in their hands, waiting quietly for the worst to happen. I was determined not to give in to that kind of despair.

My instincts were telling me now that I had to avoid feeling any sympathy for these people who were holding us captive. I remembered stories I had heard about how Chechen guerrillas would take hostages and, if the ransom money wasn't forthcoming, they would videotape themselves murdering their victims and cutting off their heads. Then they would mail the tape to those who had refused them the money. Such grisly thoughts helped remind me that we were being held by a ruthless bunch and that however extremely their people were suffering at the hands of the Russians, nothing could justify threatening to take the lives of hundreds of innocent people. Of course, those same thoughts could also have made me lose hope. But one thing I knew for sure: doing something impetuous would have been the worst possible course of action.

At about 7:00 A.M., the terrorists began bringing in cases of soft drinks and bottled water. They brought the boxes to the end of each row for us to pass along. These stocks had come, I supposed, from the buffet in the theatre's upstairs lobby, because along with the drinks, they also handed out sandwiches and pastries. To the kids in the front rows, they passed out Rafaelos—individually wrapped chocolates with a coconut filling. The odd thing was that the soft drinks and the juices were in glass bottles, which could be used as weapons. Certainly I thought about it, and when I'd finished drinking the juice, I casually stashed the bottle under the seat, though at the time I had no idea how I might use it. I would later learn I wasn't the only one to have done so.

17

THE HOUSE OF CULTURE

Thursday, October 24   8:00 A.M.

So far, we hadn't had to worry much about sanitary arrangements, but the longer the situation dragged on, the more conditions deteriorated. The terrorists couldn't have given that mundane part of their operation much thought. For most of the audience, except for those in the balcony, the bathrooms could be reached only by walking back up through the entrances and then down the stairs and through the lobby. But the lobby and the staircase leading down to the washrooms below had glass walls and everyone who passed through them would be visible from the outside. A sniper standing outside in the parking lot or on the roof of a nearby building could easily get a shot at any terrorists shepherding hostages down the stairs. If they let the hostages go by themselves, there would be nothing to stop them from simply walking out the door to freedom.

There were bathrooms on the third floor, but they couldn't accommodate all eight hundred of us. Another solution would have to be found, and in the meantime, the terrorists improvised, dealing with our needs on a case-by-case basis.

They soon realized how disruptive it was to be constantly escorting groups of hostages to the bathroom, so they limited trips to certain times of the day, and allowed none at night, when they thought the danger of a Russian attack would be greatest. Next—although I wasn't aware of any formal announcement about these arrangements—they declared that the orchestra pit would be used as a toilet, at least for the hostages on the main floor of the auditorium. It was inside the hall, so no one would have to leave or be escorted to use it, and it provided a reasonable amount of privacy.

Under normal circumstances, the orchestra pit was accessible only from the backstage area. For us to enter it that way would mean the terrorists would still have had to escort us. The only other way into it was to climb over the front partition, which stood about chest high, and then descend to the floor of the pit, about two metres below. Someone had constructed a makeshift set of steps, consisting of a chair balanced on top of a table. On the inside, where the drop was farther, they had made the same arrangement, except that instead of a chair they had used a musician's stool, something like a bar stool, set on a table.

Imagine climbing onto a table and from there onto a chair, then swinging one leg over the barrier, groping with your foot until you've found the top of the barstool, which was round and smaller and less stable than the seat of a chair, then bringing the other leg round to place the second foot on the stool, checking your balance, and then, without slipping off or tipping the stool over, climb down from the stool and table. Even without the perils that lay below, the thought of climbing into the pit was more than some hostages could bear.

Before long, the stench from the orchestra pit was overpowering, especially at the front of the auditorium, where we were sitting. The thought of going down into it was so disgusting that for a long time I tried to stave off the moment by drinking very little.

When I could hold off no longer, I stood in line, watching people struggle to climb in and then climb out again, the makeshift ladders becoming more and more treacherous and filthy all the time. Some people—older people, people who were not athletic, or those who were overweight or too frightened—could not even bring themselves to try. They were allowed to go out into the hallway where Olga's body was and fend for themselves. When my turn came, I tried to breathe as shallowly as possible—by now the stench was so bad that I almost gagged—and I climbed gingerly up and over the partition, then down, landing lightly on my feet in a few centimetres of liquid that I tried hard not to think about.

The orchestra pit was the most depressing place I had ever seen. The floor was awash in urine and feces. Music stands had tumbled over, spilling the beautiful score for *Nord-Ost* into the awful cesspool. Trying to keep their feet at least partially dry, people walked on the sheet music, treading it into the filth. There were broken, abandoned instruments lying about—cellos, violins, electric guitars, keyboards, horns, saxophones, drums—all left behind when the terrorists had driven the musicians out into the audience.

At last I understood what had excited Irina about this play when she talked about it during the intermission only a few hours ago. The music and the instruments were part of the noble, adventurous, civilized enterprise of this theatre, so full of hope and risk in its effort to rise above the misery of the past and come up with something new, a new kind of theatre. And now this enterprise lay drowned in excrement, surrounded by barbarism and death. The only concession to common decency was one the hostages came up with themselves, which was that the women would use the right side of the pit, where a small partition gave them a bit of privacy, and the men would use the left side. It was a small concession indeed.

18

THE HOUSE OF CULTURE

Thursday, October 24   9:00 A.M.

We were now anxiously awaiting our release. From our position in the front row, Irina and I could see everything that was happening on the stage. Two Chechens were pacing back and forth, pointing their guns at the audience and, occasionally, at the ceiling. Powerful flashlights were taped to the gun barrels, which they poked into ventilator shaft outlets and pointed at the rafters, playing beams of light into places where they thought people might be hiding. There was something especially frightening about this; they were like animals on the scent of prey. Occasionally they would leap off the stage, almost into our laps. They were heavy men, loaded down with lethal equipment, and the impact of them landing caused the seats, and the people in them, to shake and shudder. One of them had the word "Killer" painted on his belt, in English.

On our side of the stage sat one of the Chechen women, holding in her hand a detonator for the bombs that were on the stage. She also had a pistol, and I could tell from the way she was handling it that she wasn't used to it. She had it partly resting on her lap so that it was pointing down at the audience, in particular, at me. It was a Makarov, a weapon I'd had a passing acquaintance with in the army. Her fingers were idly playing with the trigger, and the safety catch was disengaged. I found myself staring at her, and after a while she noticed and told me to look somewhere else. But I couldn't help stealing glances at her. Her eyes were hard and vacant, and at times I could see her lips moving under her veil, as though she were talking to herself, or praying. Occasionally, she seemed about to nod off, and I fantasized about leaping up and grabbing her gun. But what then?

I found it impossible to sleep. I was too depressed by my experience in the orchestra pit, and too keyed up by the prospect of release. It was more than just a vague hope. The terrorists had talked about it; they'd examined our passports; they'd asked us to call our ambassadors; they'd given us what seemed like sensible advice and a logical explanation for their actions. Any doubts I might have had—for instance, wouldn't a large contingent of foreigners be a stronger bargaining chip with the Russian government than the Russian hostages themselves?—I dismissed. The prospect of freedom was so palpable it made me believe the terrorists were telling the truth; it made me believe they really didn't want to harm us; it made me believe Irina and I had a chance.

As I was keeping a wary eye on the woman with the pistol, Abu Bakar came onto the stage and said we should start calling our embassies to arrange for the ambassadors to come and receive us at nine o'clock. Then he and the other male terrorists disappeared behind the panels, leaving the main floor of the auditorium in the keeping of the Chechen women. From what I could see, only two men were left in the balcony, and the two very young terrorists on the stage were sitting with their backs against the wall of the proscenium, watching a small portable television set on the floor in front of them. While the others in our group called their embassies, I borrowed a cellphone (by now the battery in mine had run out), called Todor, told him briefly what was up, and asked him to call the Bulgarian ambassador again.

Dr. Shkolnikova came round and told us she'd been asked to make a list of the names and nationalities of those who were going to be released. She began at one end of the first row but seemed to be taking a long time about it. I found myself becoming incredibly irritated. "What's taking her so long?" I thought and had a ready answer: "She's Russian; she's not interested in helping us get released."

But when she came to take my name, I could see why she was so slow: her hair was limp, her face drawn, her eyes dull with fatigue. She was utterly exhausted. Like most of us, she'd been up all night but, unlike the rest of us, she'd been busy, phoning newspapers and radio stations, tending to the sick, worrying about the fate of her son, and wondering whether her husband had managed to arouse interest in the German media. I felt ashamed for feeling annoyed with her. "You must be very tired," I said.

She gave me a weak smile. "I can hardly stand up," she replied.

When she asked me where I came from, I said, "Bulgaria, but my wife is Canadian." It was an awkward moment, because it wasn't true, and, thinking ahead, I wasn't sure how the Canadian embassy would respond; at some point, I was sure Irina would be checked out and the embassy would discover the truth. We could only hope the terrorists would release her without proof of citizenship, before the truth came to light. I saw that there were already three names on the list ahead of ours: the Lows, from the United Kingdom. I recalled that if there was no Canadian embassy in a country, a Canadian could get help from a British embassy, since Canada is a member of the Commonwealth.

I thought Irina might stand a better chance if she were listed as having dual British and Canadian citizenship. But we had to come up with a good surname for her. We settled on "Cooper," after one of Irina's colleagues at English First.

It took Dr. Shkolnikova about half an hour to finish drawing up the list. Irina was still worried about how a consular official from the Canadian or the British embassy might respond to our charade, so I tried to reassure her. I simply couldn't imagine any Western diplomat, let alone a Canadian, saying in these circumstances, "Sorry, she's not one of ours," and making her go back inside the theatre to resume being a hostage. Nevertheless, it was one of those critical moments when you realize that you've set a course of action in motion, and there is no way back.

The 9 A.M. deadline drew near. Apart from our constant guard of suicide bombers, most of the terrorists were nowhere to be seen. Perhaps they were trying to get negotiations started. We now know that embassy representatives started arriving very early that morning; the Russian authorities put them in temporary headquarters in a school a few blocks from the theatre. Through Dr. Shkolnikova, a list of about sixty hostages from the Netherlands, Bulgaria, Canada, Australia, Latvia, Moldova, Yugoslavia, Belarus, Turkmenistan, Azerbaijan, Armenia, Georgia, the United States, Germany, Great Britain, Switzerland, and Ukraine was sent out. The terrorists also requested that doctors from Médecins Sans Frontières and representatives of the Red Cross come to the theatre, with the proviso that no Russians be included in any delegation.

About the same time as we were to be released, the Russian authorities used a television broadcast to appeal to the terrorists to get in touch with them, but the terrorists did not respond. Some of the hostages must have relayed a request by the terrorists to have their friends mount public demonstrations in Red Square against the war in Chechnya, because at 10:00 A.M., Red Square was closed to the public. An hour or so later, the terrorists agreed to meet with Russian journalist Anna Politkovskaya, who was in the United States to receive an award for bravery in journalism—ironically, for her coverage of the war in Chechnya. She arranged for someone to accept the award on her behalf and boarded the next available plane for Moscow.

I was only faintly aware of any of this, since we were dependent on the willingness of the Chechen women to tell us what was going on, or on what Aleksander's sister Kira was able to pass on from the radio broadcasts she was listening to. Occasionally we would hear bits of conversations between the terrorists, carried on loudly and in Russian for our benefit. At one point, I heard one terrorist remark scornfully that Russian officials had contacted them and offered money. "We don't want money," was his response. "We want freedom." And when someone asked them what the offer had been, he said, "A million dollars," and laughed. From what I knew of the hostage trade in Chechnya, this was no more than chump change.

Time passed and nothing happened. It was now well past 9:00 A.M. We knew that our ambassadors or their representatives were outside the theatre, so the fact that we hadn't been released yet alarmed us. None of the male terrorists would pay any attention to us, and none of the women seemed to know anything, or if they did, they were unwilling to tell us. Whenever any of the male hostage-takers appeared in the hall, we would remind them that our diplomats were waiting for us outside, but they would either ignore us or brush us off.

At about noon, they told us that they were not going to release us. The only reason they would give was that our ambassadors had not complied with their conditions. Irina slumped back in her seat. I felt numb.

Despite the deep disappointment within our small group, no one caused a fuss, though Natalia wept audibly while her son tried to comfort her. The Ukrainian woman beside me was extremely upset and a short time later, I noticed that she had gone, probably to rejoin her nephew on the other side of the theatre.

Why had they refused to release us? Could it have been some reluctance on the Russian government's part? After all, the hostage-taking was potentially harmful to the President Putin, who, in the face of international criticism, had been promoting his policy toward Chechnya as part of the war on terror. As long as foreigners were inside the building, captives of Chechen terrorists, he could present his problem as an international crisis that merited the attention, sympathy, and forbearance of the rest of the world, especially of the US. I wasn't sure about public opinion in the US, but I knew that many Canadians who were aware of the wars in Chechnya tended to sympathize with the Chechens, as the underdog. Now all that would change. Putin could point out that there were American, Dutch, British, Canadian, and Swiss victims of terror as well. If the terrorists let us go, however, we wouldn't be victims any longer. So, perhaps ungenerously, I felt that the Russian agenda had played a part in the failed release.

On the other hand, the Russian hostages must have heaved a sigh of relief that we were still there. Why? Because they believed that once the foreign hostages were out of the theatre, the Russian Special Forces would no longer hesitate to come in shooting, risking all their lives for a quick settlement of the crisis. As long as the foreign hostages remained captives, the Russian hostages could feel they still had a chance.

So here we were, caught in the middle. Clearly, our ordeal was far from over. More than twelve hours had passed and the terrorists were only now agreeing to talk with certain people. I took it as a good sign that they were willing to talk to some Russians, at least to Anna Politkovskaya, the journalist, and to Iosif Kobzon, a singer and member of the Duma, as well as to representatives of the Yabloko Party, a liberal faction in the Duma. These were all Russians who had argued publicly for a peaceful settlement of the Chechen war, and I hoped they might persuade the terrorists to let at least some of us go. What the terrorists wanted more than anything else, I believed, was a way of conveying their message to the rest of the world. Once they had done that, their determination to blow themselves and the rest of us up might diminish.

Because they hadn't released us, we were back to where we had started, and all I could do was think hard about our situation and how to improve it. I didn't have any brilliant ideas, but I did discover in myself a hardening determination not to give in to despair. As Irina said later, there was no way back, so you could only go forward, even if you didn't know which way was forward—or if there was a way forward at all. If there was an unspoken solidarity among the hostages, that was its essence. That, and the fear of death.

19

CHECHNYA

2002

In Chechnya, there is a thriving trade in corpses.

Imagine that the Russians pick up a man on one of their periodic sweeps or mop-up operations through a rural district. It's meant to "cleanse" the place of rebels, but it is also a form of terrorism. Armed, masked men travelling in armoured vehicles arrive at the man's door late at night, enter without permission, smash the furniture, sweep the chinaware onto the floor, break windows, threaten to rape his wife, then drag him outside, perhaps taking with them the one thing of value in the house: an Afghan rug, a television set. For good measure, they bash in the side window of the old Moskvitch parked in the yard, pour gasoline inside the car, and toss in a match.

In the morning, the woman begins a frantic search for her husband. She visits makeshift detention centres, grimy police stations, crowded prisons, holding camps, and morgues. The authorities are stone-faced. He is not here, they say. We have no record of his detention. The woman goes to the local hospital, but the staff are exhausted and overworked and scarcely have time to deal with her. They have no medicine, they haven't been paid in months, and the beds are full of people with their arms and legs blown off by ordnance. The staff have to take up collections in order to buy anesthetics; they perform operations under the constant threat of power outages. The woman asks friends and acquaintances if they know where her husband might be; after more than a decade of conflict in Chechnya, thousands of mothers, wives, sisters, and daughters are searching for sons, husbands, brothers, and fathers. Sometimes the missing are still children. But what is childhood, in Chechnya? Even children can carry guns.

Time goes by, hope fades. She realizes her husband may never come back. But without a body, how can one be sure? There is nothing worse than not knowing, nothing worse than not burying the dead. Death comes to everyone, eventually; it's natural, a part of life. Even violent death is the will of Allah. But disappearance? No body, no last remains, no final proof—the dishonour of that is almost harder to cope with than death itself.

One evening a man shows up at her door. He's wearing a suit and tie and carrying a briefcase. He's heard of her trouble, he says. Perhaps he can help. Warily, the woman invites him in. There is not much food in the house, so she offers him a cup of tea.

"I have information," the man says. "I have heard that your husband was held for a while in a detention camp." He pauses, waiting for a response. There is nothing to say. "Yes, I know," he goes on, "this is not good news. Not many are released, and those that are—well . . . " He pauses. "But," he sighs, "they have found bodies. They're not far from the camp."

"Do you think . . . ?" the woman asks.

"It may be," he said. "There is only one way to find out."

"What should I do?"

"Tell me how to identify him and I can arrange for you to receive the body." He waits for her to ask the question.

"How much will you need?" she says finally.

He names a figure. It is more money than the family can raise. He studies the woman's face, then says: "There is another way that is less costly, though I warn you, it is not pleasant."

Not pleasant? What could be more unpleasant than this? "Tell me."

"I can arrange for you to go to the site yourself to look for him. There are no guarantees that you will find him, of course, but no hassles from the Russians either."

"And . . ."

He names another figure. It is still outrageous, but if the rest of the family helps, it can be raised.

She agrees. What else can she do? She tells him she will need time to get the money.

"There is very little time," he says. "You see, the bodies are not yet buried. Soon they must make a grave."

He sees the despair in her eyes. "Look," he says. "I know of your family. I'm told you are honourable people. Give me your word, and I will give you a week to raise the money. In the meantime, I will arrange for you to go there and look."

Early the next morning, he is back with a car to drive her to the site. It is in a large meadow that rises gently toward the rugged mountains in the distance. It's a bitterly clear late October day in the year 2000. He pulls up to a farm gate, gets out of the car, opens the door for her, then walks over to some guards in Russian uniforms. They are huddled in a group, Kalashnikovs on their shoulders, smoking. He says something—perhaps he gives them some money—and they gesture her through.

Inside the gate are muddy ruts in the soft ground made by heavy trucks. They follow the ruts deeper into the field. After about ninety metres, the ruts diverge. There were several trucks, each one driven to a different part of the field. The woman stops to look around. In the distance she can see a small group of people gathered around what look like mounds of earth. She walks toward the nearest one, afraid of what she will find. It is exactly what she thought—human corpses, a tangle of limbs and torsos, dumped on the ground like a load of fire-wood. There are other women there, looking on with anguished faces.

She can hardly stand to look, but she must. The bodies are stiff, blood from their wounds dried and caked on their skin and clothing, matting their hair, faces frozen in grimaces of fear and agony, eyes half open, teeth bared. Some of the corpses are mutilated, as if by torture.

A cold breeze is blowing down from the mountains, mercifully carrying away the stench of death. Now and then she hears another woman wail in recognition, a long, agonizing keening.

And then he's at her side, the man in the suit. "Come with me," he says, as though he understands. He takes her by the elbow and leads her across the field to a row of bodies laid out in a rough row near a stone fence. She sees the familiar blue shirt, the shock of black hair, the beard. He's lying partly on one side, his face turned away, one of his legs twisted underneath him. The other foot is bare, with burn marks on the sole. There is a bullet hole in his temple.

"I will bring him home to you later," says a voice in her ear.

20

THE HOUSE OF CULTURE

Thursday, October 24   1:00 P.M.

Our only hope now was that a deal could be worked out between the Russian authorities and the terrorists. I didn't think the prospects were good. The terrorists were growing more and more agitated as the day wore on. The Chechen women remained impassively at their posts, but the men seemed constantly in motion, coming and going, gathering in small huddles to confer, then heading back outside the room, as though there were matters of great importance going on elsewhere. Since our lives depended on their mood, we were anxious to know what was happening, but they refused to answer our questions. Occasionally, they would encourage each other by chanting *"Allahu akhbar"* together like a chorus of cheerleaders.

From their behaviour and the occasional overheard remarks, I decided that whatever negotiations had taken place hadn't accomplished

111

much, mainly because, as far as we knew, they hadn't talked with anyone who had the authority to grant them anything. We would see Movsar on the telephone, pacing back and forth on the apron of the stage like a caged beast, seething with anger and frustration. That afternoon, he sent Dr. Shkolnikova outside to deliver a message to the media. "The Chechens are starting to get impatient with us," she told journalists. "They say, 'Your government is doing nothing to help you.' We want to know: Where is Putin? Has he spoken? If our troops are not withdrawn from Chechnya soon, they say they will start shooting us."

When Putin finally did speak, in a televised address to the nation in the mid-afternoon on Thursday, Kira heard excerpts on her radio and told us that he'd described the hostage-taking as one of the largest terrorist attacks in history, and gone on to say that the raids were not planned in Chechnya, but "in one of the foreign terrorist centres." It was a comment meant mainly for American ears; his remarks did nothing to ease the tensions inside the theatre.

A short time later we heard that Al-Jazeera, the Qatar-based Arab television station that has become a kind of messenger service for terrorists and dictators in hiding, broadcast a tape that it claimed had been dropped off anonymously at its Moscow offices earlier that day. The tape, which I saw parts of later, shows Movsar Barayev sitting in front of a laptop. "We've come to Russia's capital city to stop the war or die for Allah," he says. The tape then shows a group of women terrorists with their faces covered. Behind them is a dark banner with white Arabic script, perhaps the very same banner they hung above the stage in the theatre. One of the women says, "We might as well die here as in Chechnya. Here we will die taking hundreds of unbelievers with us." Then the tape cuts back to Barayev, who says, in a flat, emotionless voice: "I swear to Allah we desire death more than they desire life. Allah is great!"

Whatever the intention of the tape, broadcasting it after Putin made his address had the effect of reinforcing his claim that the terrorists were Muslim fundamentalists aligning themselves with a wider Islamic jihad, effectively putting them beyond the pale as negotiating partners. But I noticed something else: as I watched the terrorists on their cellphones, I got the distinct impression that they were not really interested in negotiating, certainly not with anyone less than President Putin himself. But there was more: I began to wonder if they were acting on their own, or if they were taking orders from someone outside. I remembered that the previous night a man suddenly appeared in the theatre; what was striking about him was that he wore a suit, rather than camouflage gear, and all the terrorists seemed to know him. The men cheered when they saw him and some of the women joined in. It was a chilling sight. This man had made it through the police lines, yet he was clearly one of the terrorists. They were speaking in Russian, and I managed to overhear a bit of their conversation.

"Was everything normal?" one of the Chechens asked him in Russian.

"Of course," he replied. "Fifty rubles here, fifty rubles there. I came in the normal way."

The thought that someone on the terrorists' side could have bribed his way past the cordon of police officers and soldiers around the theatre should have shocked me more than it did. But corruption is still a fact of life in Russia. A cop stops you on the street to check your ID card and thinks he's found something wrong with it. Five hundred rubles will make the problem go away. Or a traffic cop pulls you over for a safety check and you know he'll find something wrong with your car. What's the solution? Rubles.

It gets worse. Suppose you're on a wanted list and wish to conceal your real name, and certainly the fact that you're of Chechen nationality. The best solution is to get a new internal passport. To buy one on the black market will cost you between US$1,000 and US$1,500 in Moscow, maybe more in Chechnya. And what you get is the real thing; not a counterfeit pass or a forgery, but a genuine document that bestows a new identity on you, one with no flaws to tip off the authorities, one with your own picture in it, one that would fool anyone.

And so the internal passport, the very thing that's supposed to make it hard for people to fool the authorities, becomes a tool of deception that is all but impossible to detect. And with a corrupt police force, even if you are detected, you can almost always buy your way out of trouble. So the questions that interested me most were not how these Chechens managed to travel the two thousand kilometres to Moscow, passing through countless checkpoints along the way; or where they got their weapons; or how they managed to stay undetected in Moscow, a city in which the police or the neighbours are constantly on the alert for suspicious individuals; or how they got so close to the theatre with so many weapons and explosives without being caught; or even how they were still getting through the heavily armed police lines outside and entering the theatre. The real questions were, Whose side were the police really on? How could we trust them if, even now, a terrorist could enter the building with ease? Were the authorities the solution, or part of the problem?

At one point, when it was obvious that negotiations were going nowhere, I approached one of the terrorists—I think it was Yassir. I told him that I had heard on the radio that the United Nations was preparing to pass a resolution on Chechnya. It wasn't true, but I thought it was worth a try. "Why do you want to spoil your image in the West at this crucial moment? The West was with you. If you release the foreigners, you will win back support."

He looked at me and said simply: "We are only obeying orders."

I was taken aback. Did he mean that their orders came from outside the building, from somewhere in Moscow, or Chechnya? Or did he mean what Putin was suggesting, that their orders came from beyond Chechnya, from Afghanistan or Saudi Arabia or Yemen or somewhere else in the Muslim world? And did this mean that they had an international network—a source of money, arms, solidarity, intelligence, and instructions? Whatever it was, if someone outside this building was giving them orders and advice, it made our plight that much more dangerous.

21

CHECHNYA

1991–2002

Kidnapping and hostage-taking have long been stock-in-trade for Chechen bandits, but as military tactics, they have come into their own during the recent conflict with Russia. The distinction between political hostage-taking and kidnapping for money became blurred in the mid-1990s as vast sums, procured as ransom, were used to finance the Chechen rebel cause and underwrite the secessionist movement. One report suggests that Chechen soldiers expected to draw wages only after a successful hostage-taking had produced enough ransom money to pay them.

After Chechnya declared independence in 1991, there were at least eight major hostage-taking incidents, starting with the hijacking of Flight 2154 in Mineralnye Vody, a resort town in the North Caucasus, by Shamil Basayev, the mastermind behind the notorious hostage-taking at Budennovsk. In August 1992, another plane was hijacked on the Grozny–Moscow route by a lone Chechen armed with a grenade who demanded that the plane change course for Turkey. While refuelling in Moscow, the plane was stormed and the hostage-taker killed. None of the passengers was hurt.

Then in May 1994, four Chechens hijacked an excursion bus in Stavropol filled with Russian school children and their parents and teachers—thirty hostages in all. The terrorists demanded a helicopter, fuel, and US$10 million. After tense negotiations, they released all the children and some of the adults. The following day, a helicopter was provided and the terrorists took off for Dagestan. Bad weather forced them to land in Chechnya, where the terrorists were quickly taken into custody. None of the hostages was hurt.

The following month, another helicopter was hijacked. This time, when the Russian Special Forces stormed the aircraft, the Chechens detonated a grenade, killing five people.

Six and a half months after Shamil Basayev took the hospital in Budennovsk, on January 9, 1996, a band of Chechen fighters led by Salman Raduyev attempted to take a Russian military airfield near the town of Kizlyar in Dagestan. When they were beaten back, they entered the town, captured around two thousand hostages, and took over the municipal hospital and a nine-storey apartment building nearby, in effect holding the entire town to ransom. The reasons for the raid were unclear but probably involved murky intra-Chechen politics. At the outset, Raduyev vowed to fight to the death and to "turn this city to hell and ashes." Yet the same day, he and his men left Kizlyar for Chechnya in buses, taking about one hundred and sixty hostages with them. The Russians, despite promising them safe passage, attacked the convoy at the border village of Pervomaiskoye. The Chechens entered the village, took more hostages, and for three days held off a full-scale Russian onslaught involving thousands of soldiers backed up with helicopter gunships and artillery, weaponry that virtually guaranteed civilian casualties. Indeed, over a dozen hostages were killed in the siege, along with twenty-six Russian soldiers and a large number of Chechens. The event prompted the hijacking of a Turkish Black Sea ferry by Turkish sympathizers with the Chechen cause, who threatened to destroy the boat unless the Russians lifted the siege in Pervomaiskoye and let the Chechens go. The incident was settled peacefully. Mysteriously, the Chechens managed to slip away in the night and escape across the Aksai River into Chechnya. There is still speculation that the Russians had simply let them go.

During the second Chechen war, there were a few minor incidents of hostage-taking, one involving an airliner that was hijacked to Saudi Arabia (the terrorists were captured, but given short prison sentences), the other involving a bus, in which no one was killed. In almost all such incidents, while ransom money was sometimes a factor, the objectives were mainly military. Between the two wars, however, the mercenary spirit came to prevail over the military. One of the most barbaric and notorious practitioners of the black art of hostage-taking for profit, and possibly for more nefarious ends, was Arbi Barayev.

Arbi Barayev was a warlord who wrapped himself in Wahhabism and commanded a ruthless brigade of Islamic guerrillas known more for their cruelty and the use of torture than for their fidelity to Islam. One particularly grisly incident attributed to them was the capture, in October 1998, of four Western telecommunications workers, three Britons and one New Zealander, all of whom were working for Granger Telecom, a British telephone company hired by the Mashkhadov government to help establish a decent telephone system in Chechnya. The four men were living in Grozny and were supposed to have been given lodging in a secure compound, with gates and armed guards. Instead, they were quartered in a house that was exposed to the street on two sides. In the early morning of October 3, 1998, the house was surrounded by twenty armed men, who took them hostage.

In captivity, the four men were accused of being spies and beaten badly almost every other day. According to eyewitness accounts, they were frequently shown videos of the dead bodies of other victims, as well as videos of some their captors' victims being murdered. Their captors' purpose was evidently to have them confess to being agents of the British and Israeli governments, and of working to stop the spread of Islam in the region.

Some hope was held out for their release before Christmas, but that hope was shattered on December 8, when a bag was found on the roadside about forty kilometres south of Grozny. It contained the severed heads of all four men. Maskhadov immediately blamed the deed on "outside forces" intent on undermining Chechnya's budding independence. But Arbi Barayev and his gang were rumoured to have been behind it. Some of those rumours have it that Osama bin Laden himself offered Barayev more money to kill the telecommunications workers than he might have gained had their company paid the ransom. But such stories don't ring true: it doesn't take an al Qaeda connection to explain the grisly act.

Much of what is claimed about Arbi Barayev is conjectural, but there were persistent allegations that he had connections to the Russian Security Service, the FSB; that he may have had a hand in the apartment bombings that terrorized Muscovites in the late summer of 1999 and that led directly to the second Chechen war; and that he was something of a double agent, working for both the Russians and the Chechens. The truth will probably never be known: he was killed by the Russians in the summer of 2001.

In a sense, Movsar Barayev inherited the family business. Arbi Barayev was the brother of Movsar's mother, and when Uncle Arbi died, Movsar, whose real surname was Suliemenov, assumed his mother's maiden name as an act of piety, took command of his Islamic fighters, and donned the mantle of a warrior leader. The Barayev family claimed other distinctions, too. Arbi's sister, Khava Barayeva, who was also Movsar's aunt, blew herself up at the age of nineteen in an attack on a Russian military base. Arbi Barayev's widow, Zura, was said to be among the women terrorists at the House of Culture.

When he had been in command of the Islamic brigade for less than a year, Movsar Barayev disappeared. There were rumours of his death, and twice before October 2002, the Russians claimed to have killed him, the last time a mere two weeks before he appeared on stage at the House of Culture in Moscow.

22

THE HOUSE OF CULTURE

Thursday, October 24   5:00 P.M.

It had now been almost twenty hours since we had been taken hostage, and some of the hostages were beginning to experience serious health problems. Peter Low, the Englishman who was in Moscow with his wife to visit their son Richard, had a heart condition. After successfully pleading with the terrorists to be released, he was let go. His wife and son remained behind.

Then Igor, the director of the Irish dance troupe, suddenly developed terrible pains in his abdomen. Irina and I were by this time at the front of the theatre, but we could hear him moaning at the back, and when we looked around, we saw Dr. Shkolnikova tending to him, wrapping him in a blanket and laying him on the floor in the aisle. She went to Movsar and told him that Igor probably had a ruptured appendix and needed immediate treatment. At first,

Movsar appeared to agree to this. With the help of some of the students, Dr. Shkolnikova managed to get Igor to his feet. She was supporting him, his arm over her shoulder, as they moved up the aisle toward the rear exit, when Movsar suddenly shouted, "Stop! You're faking it!"

Dr. Shkolnikova stood her ground. "On the contrary," she said, "this is a serious situation. If you don't let him go, he'll die."

"In that case, we'll just shoot him," Movsar said. He pushed Dr. Shkolnikova out of the way. Igor fell down, and Movsar began kicking him viciously in the stomach, yelling something in Chechen, as Igor cried out in pain. Then Movsar beckoned to one of his men, who dragged Igor, by now unconscious, out of the auditorium. We waited, terrified, for shots, but heard nothing.

The following day, Movsar was at one point standing near us at the front of the theatre and I heard him say to one of the Chechens, in Russian so that we would understand, "You should check out this guy with appendicitis. Maybe he's dead already, but you should check him anyway." It was Movsar's sick way of letting us know that Igor hadn't been shot.

If, on the one hand, the terrorists behaved callously toward us, there were some ways in which they respected our needs. Several times, staff members of the International Red Cross were allowed into the auditorium, bringing with them medicine and first-aid kits. The women hostage-takers, too, often proved surprisingly helpful; they distributed tampons to the women who needed them, and pills to those with heart conditions and high blood pressure. They even brought us more juice from the concession. I had to keep reminding myself, though, that these acts of kindness were all taking place inside one colossal act of unkindness, one that undermined the significance of all the good they did.

One terrorist was particularly aggressive; Movsar had warned us not to cross him because, he said, "He is the most merciless of us all." This man didn't carry an AK-47 as the others did; he was armed only with a pistol, which he had a habit of waving about with a sadistic flourish. The day before, he had decided to have some fun. Having found a box of individually wrapped chocolates, he jumped onto the stage and tossed them into the rows of Russian hostages. But as hungry as the hostages must have been, they did not humiliate themselves by crawling around the floor for a candy. It was an impressive display of self-control by the Russians, who had every reason to feel a far greater despair than did we.

Sitting in the front row, with the Chechens chafing at the slow progress of negotiations, Irina and I felt more vulnerable than when we had been sitting at the back of the theatre. The bombs taped to chairs on stage were no more than a metre or so away. The woman suicide bomber with the detonator was still sitting right in front of us, still waving her gun in our direction. And every few minutes, it seemed, one of the male hostage-takers would jump off the stage, landing almost in our laps.

To make matters worse, we were close to the orchestra pit. It wasn't just the smell that bothered us; the people waiting to use the "facilities" were lined up across the front of the theatre in the narrow space between the front row and the stage, and were virtually standing on our feet. We had to try to move.

As people lined up to use the orchestra pit, there was a kind of musical-chairs confusion, and I was able to slip into a seat beside the actor who played the romantic lead, Sanya, sitting a few places down the row. He was a young man about my age, still wearing his makeup and costume, a World War II pilot's uniform that was so realistic I felt, for a fleeting moment, that I was in the presence of a real captain.

Leaning closely toward him and speaking quietly, I got straight to the point: "I need to know something about the layout of the theatre."

He looked at me and smiled faintly. "Go ahead," he said. "You have any bright ideas?"

"Those double doors on the left side," I said. They were the same doors Olga had been pushed through just before she was shot. "If things started happening, could we escape that way?"

He thought for a moment. "If you get through the door," he whispered, "you'll be in the corridor. The door on your right goes into the backstage area—but they control that, I think. If you go left, you end up in the entrance foyer and the cloakroom."

"And straight ahead?"

"Glass windows, floor to ceiling."

"Would they be hard to break?"

"I think it's safety glass."

"But you could break it?"

"With something heavy."

"What's on the other side?"

"A kind of courtyard. But it's fenced in."

"But maybe these guys don't control it."

"Maybe not. Are you . . . ?"

"I don't know. It helps to know this. Thanks."

I went back to my seat, hoping that no one had noticed our conversation. If the police stormed the theatre, or if the hostage-takers decided—or were told—to blow the place up, we might, if we were closer to this door and still alive, have a slim chance of breaking out of the theatre before it collapsed. I whispered what I had learned to Irina. "I'm going to try to move back a few rows," I said. "Then we'll be in a better position."

"How will you do that?" she asked.

"I'm not sure yet, but there's so much going on with these lineups for the bathroom, they might not notice. Let's just wait for a chance."

"Are you sure it's the right thing to do?"

"I have to do something. I'm going crazy just sitting here. Besides, that woman is always pointing her gun in our direction. Do we need a better reason?"

"Just be careful. Don't draw attention to yourself."

At about 5:00 P.M., a ripple of excitement went through the audience. Two doctors had entered the theatre from the outside. One was Dr. Leonid Roshal, a famous pediatrician who was also chairman of the International Committee for Paediatric Disasters; the other was a Jordanian doctor, a colleague of his. The two of them spent over six hours inside the auditorium, and I caught occasional glimpses of them moving through the audience, talking to hostages, handing out medicines and sanitary products, and assessing the hostages' state of mind and health, paying particular attention to the remaining children. I overheard bits of conversation as Dr. Roshal argued strongly for the release of more children. About an hour after he arrived, Dr. Roshal persuaded the terrorists to let him take out the body of Olga Romanova, which had lain in the hallway for over twelve hours. Television cameras caught the two doctors dragging her corpse out the front door between them, the first casualty of the hostage-taking.

I decided to make the move to change our position. I would wait for a moment when a lot of people were lining up to use the orchestra pit, get in line myself, and then when I was finished, simply not return to my seat. If I managed to pull it off, Irina could do the same.

When I finally climbed back out of the orchestra pit, I tried to wipe the worst of the mess off my shoes on the carpet while working my way back along the long lineup to my seat in the front row. When I reached my seat, I continued easing myself down the queue until I reached the end of the row. Then, as casually as I could, I walked up the aisle to the fifth row and took another seat close to the end. No one said a word; no one tried to stop me; perhaps no one even noticed me. The woman standing guard farther up the aisle, the only one who might have seen that I didn't belong in that row, appeared to be paying no attention.

Soon Irina joined me, and then Aleksander. We were now a few rows farther away from the guard on the stage, and the closest suicide bomber was a couple of rows away on the far side, which made it easier to talk among ourselves. I had already told Aleksander what I had learned from the actor and he'd agreed that in an emergency it might be worth trying to escape through the window, even though breaking the glass might be difficult. In general, however, Aleksander's approach was to wait patiently until something happened. I sensed that he felt it was better to bide our time than to make any grandiose plans.

But it wasn't in my nature to bide my time. I had another glass juice bottle and I stashed it away for future use. I tried to visualize taking the gun from the suicide bomber closest to us, releasing the safety catch, at the same time tearing the battery off her belt, disabling her bomb. But what then? Would I grab Irina and bolt for the door, try to duck out before they shot us, then use the gun to smash the window? As I ran through the scenario in my mind, it seemed far-fetched. I felt Irina nudge me.

"Stop looking at her!" she whispered.

"Is it that obvious?" I replied, turning back away from the guard and looking down at the floor.

"Of course. She's getting irritated."

"But I can't just sit here."

I needed to take a closer look at the door. I started to get out of my seat but felt Irina tugging at me to sit down. "I have to do something," I said.

I looked at the women who was guarding us, made an apologetic gesture, and stepped into the aisle. I saw a woman's handbag leaning against the wall by the double doors and bent down to pick it up. I could feel the guard becoming alert.

"Is this yours?" I asked Irina, holding up the bag.

"No, I have mine right here," she said. I could tell she was frightened, but not by the terrorists. "Come back and sit down," she said firmly to me.

I glanced at the guard, shrugged my shoulders as if to say, I guess I was wrong, and returned to my seat.

"You scared me to death," Irina whispered.

A few moments later there was a terrific explosion and the sound of gunfire coming from inside the building. People screamed and we scrambled under our seats—or tried to. Was this the moment we'd all been dreading? For what seemed like a long time, nothing happened. Later, one of the Chechen women told us that two girls had tried to escape and had been shot, along with two police officers who came to help them.

Two teenaged girls being held in the balcony had indeed escaped by jumping out a window on the third floor. They had noticed that in the third-floor bathroom, which was being used by the hostages held in the balcony, was a large casement window that could be opened. Directly beneath it, one floor below, was a small concrete canopy sheltering a service entrance. The girls also noticed that the guard generally stayed outside the bathroom.

It was a highly risky move—one that easily could have cost them their lives—and they weren't able to work up the courage to act until this evening, when the situation had become so tense that they were convinced that either the terrorists would start shooting hostages or the Special Forces would storm the building. The dangers either way were so great that they felt they had nothing to lose. So with this in mind, they asked to be escorted to the bathroom.

As the girls had hoped, their guard took them to the door and let them go in unaccompanied. Some people were already in the bathroom with

their children, and the two girls asked them to close the door behind
them when they left. The minute they were alone, the girls opened the
window and, one after the other, jumped out into the darkness.

Two Special Forces officers monitoring that side of the theatre
saw the girls jump and ran over to assist them. While an officer was
helping one of the girls, who had hurt her ankle when she landed, off
the canopy, the Chechen guard became suspicious. He went inside,
saw the open window, realized what had happened, and started shooting out of the window. He may even have thrown a grenade. He
wounded one of the soldiers, but by this time both girls had been
whisked to safety around the corner.

The guard's leg was bleeding badly. The Special Forces members
who were listening to conversations inside the theatre through the
planted microphones heard him rush into the auditorium shouting,
"If I've been wounded by a bullet, I'll kill you all." As it turned out,
he'd been cut by a piece of falling glass, and he merely fired his gun
into the air a few times to let off steam.

W hen the shooting stopped, we got up off the floor and back into
our seats. The terrorists had become busy on the stage, setting up
what appeared to be flash guns or strobe lights aimed at the audience.
Irina thought this was part of their preparation for an attack: when
the storming began, she speculated, they would turn off the house
lights and ignite the flashes to blind and confuse the attackers, giving
the terrorists time to coordinate the destruction of the building.
Whatever the lights were for, the terrorists were definitely getting
ready for something.

Late that afternoon, they had released Dr. Shkolnikova. It may have
been part of the understanding the terrorists had with her, since her
husband had contacted the German media as he said he would and

her own dramatic and vivid accounts, via cellphone, of conditions inside the theatre had been broadcast live throughout Moscow and quoted in the international press. No one had worked harder to make sure the Russian authorities understood the dangers we were facing inside the theatre, and this in itself put greater pressure on those authorities to take our lives into account.

But that was the very reason why her release made me uneasy. Why had the terrorists chosen this moment to let her go? Had they sent her out on one last desperate mission to dissuade the authorities from an attack they knew was coming? Or had they given her amnesty from the terrible death they were about to inflict on those of us who remained?

Another disquieting sign was that the Chechens took down the Arabic banners they had hung at the front of the theatre and in the balcony. It was as though they were packing up before leaving, perhaps fearing that the banners would be desecrated in a raid. They removed a similar flag wrapped around the large bomb they'd planted at the centre of the balcony seats. I could hear shouting—what sounded like commands— coming from behind the panels that hid part of the stage.

One of the women locked the exit nearest us with a key, which she then slipped into her pocket. My heart sank as I realized she had blocked our one possible avenue of escape. Next, a large group of male terrorists appeared on the stage, gesturing wildly and shouting in Chechen. One of the terrorists standing in the balcony yelled out, "They've decided to storm the theatre. Say goodbye to each other."

It was about 8:00 P.M. With cries of "There's going to be war!" Movsar, waving his AK-47 like a pointer, ordered us all to move toward the centre of the theatre where the largest bomb was propped up on one of the seats. It looked almost harmless, like a fat water tank about to topple over on its side, but there were those two ominous wires hanging out of it leading to the detonator, which was held by one of the women sitting next to it.

We were stunned, and responded to Movsar's order slowly and reluctantly. Most of us were exhausted and deeply discouraged. Many appeared to have given up hope. Irina and I were near the end of our row and as people began to move to the centre, we tried our best to keep our position on the outside of the pack. Again, it probably didn't matter much, but we felt some small comfort in keeping our distance from the bomb.

By this time, most of the terrorists, including the women suicide bombers, had gathered in the auditorium. The women moved as close to us and to each other as they could, forming a perimeter around us, as though we might try to break free and escape. It was one of the few times that all the terrorists appeared to be in the same room at once, though I knew others must have been posted outside the auditorium. People began again to make calls on their cellphones, pleading with those outside to urge the Russians not to do anything. Many were weeping, some were simply sitting with their heads down, praying.

Then one of the terrorists ordered us to get under our seats, and without thinking, we all got down, covered our heads with our hands, and waited. It didn't occur to me at the time what a ridiculous order it was. The whole point of having us gather round the bomb was to make sure that we would die instantly. Why then were they ordering us to take shelter? Shelter from what?

I think this was the moment I finally believed—or rather I knew, because it was something I felt in my bones—that I would not survive. I kept hearing in my head that infernal slogan, "We want to die more than you want to live"—the one they repeated at every opportunity, reminding us of it, rubbing it in. It was meant to demoralize us, and it was finally beginning to work.

The children huddled on the floor with us must have felt even more helpless and terrified. I remembered peeking into the rehearsal rooms on the third floor during the intermission—long ago now, in another

The second act of *Nord-Ost* opened with an exuberant dance by Russian pilot cadets and mechanics, seen here in a production shot. At 9:05 P.M. on October 23, 2002, Chechen terrorists leaped onto the stage of the Moscow theatre and demanded an end to the war in Chechnya.

Shortly after the news of the hostage-taking broke, troops from the Federal Security Service, the army, and the Moscow police force arrived on the scene. Alpha Squad snipers (above) were deployed around the theatre.

Eighteen of the fifty Chechen hostage-takers were women. They had bombs strapped around their waists and were armed with pistols and grenades. Their oft-repeated slogan was "We want to die more than you want to live."

(Associated Press/NTV Russian Channel)

(Reuters NewMedia Inc./CORBIS/Magmaphoto.com)

This homemade bomb—the gas tank of a truck stuffed with an artillery shell surrounded by nails, ball bearings, and metal fragments—was placed in the middle of the theatre among the hostages. According to Russian bomb experts, it was powerful enough to bring down the entire building.

In this shot, taken from a video made by the terrorists,
the hostages line up awaiting their turn to climb down
into the orchestra pit, which became an improvised latrine.

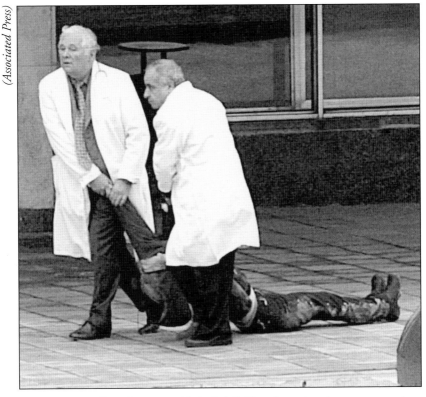

The terrorists allowed Dr. Leonid Roshal (left) and another doctor to attend to
the needs of the hostages, many of whom were children. They were permitted
to remove the body of Olga Romanova, a young woman shot by the terrorists
when she encouraged the hostages to revolt against their captors.

Dr. Maria Shkolnikova, a well-known Moscow pediatrician, was in the audience when the Chechens took over the theatre. She is shown here leaving the theatre carrying written messages from the hostages to their loved ones.

On Friday, October 25, the terrorists gave an interview to NTV, a private Russian television network. On the right is the apparent leader of the group, Movsar Barayev, flanked by an unidentified terrorist. The interview was broadcast without sound.

Relatives of the hostages organized demonstrations calling on the Russian
government to withdraw the army from Chechnya and negotiate
with the terrorists. Here, cast members who had not been performing
that night marched and sang songs from the musical.

On October 26, a man claiming to be the father of a young boy who
had been taken hostage entered the theatre. The terrorists shot him,
and his body was later placed on the steps outside the theatre. He was
one of four people shot by the terrorists during the fifty-seven-hour siege.

(Alexandre Korolkov)

At about 5:00 A.M. on Saturday, October 26, the Russian Special Forces introduced an as yet unidentified knock-out gas into the theatre. After waiting until they were certain most of the people inside were unconscious, the Russian forces then swiftly penetrated the theatre in an attempt to secure the building before the terrorists had a chance to blow it up.

(Associated Press/NTV Russian Channel)

The Russian Special Forces killed all or most of the hostage-takers. In this picture, taken from a television image, the bodies of several women suicide bombers are seen with bombs still strapped around their waists. It remains a mystery why the women failed to detonate their explosives.

When the terrorists had been subdued, the Special Forces
and other workers began bringing out the hostages who
had been overcome by the gas. Not enough doctors or
paramedics were on hand, and those who were did not
know what the proper treatment should be.

The scene outside the House of Culture at dawn, Saturday, October 26.
The theatre was cleared of hostages; the only signs of the siege
were the huge tears in the *Nord-Ost* banner.

(Associated Press)

Most of the liberated hostages, still unconscious, were taken to hospital by bus.
Of the nearly eight hundred people taken captive by the Chechen terrorists,
129 died as a result of the rescue operation, mostly from respiratory
difficulties caused by the drug or its after-effects.

(Alexandre Korolkov)

The deaths of two of the
young actors, Arsenyi, thirteen,
and Kristina, fourteen, moved
many Muscovites. The city's
mayor decreed that they be
buried together in a famous
cemetery alongside some of
Russia's most distinguished
musicians and artists. A young
mourner at the funeral holds
a picture of Kristina.

life—seeing kids in cat costumes practising dance routines, or singing choruses from *Nord-Ost,* or learning how to tap dance, and feeling their enthusiasm and the dedication of their teachers. They were here because their parents wanted them to have these opportunities, or because they wanted them to see this play and catch some of its spirit. Did they feel the same certainty I did that they were about to die? And had the terrorists chosen this theatre, this play, because they knew there would be children in the audience?

I felt an almost uncontrollable rage at this intrusion of violence and cruelty and death into the lives of so many people who did not deserve it. Yes, there had been moments when I had begun to believe that there must have been good reasons for the Chechens to take such extreme measures. But it wasn't the men—the Movsars and the Abu Bakars and the Yassirs—who had made me see things that way, but the women, the black widows wrapped in their dark shawls and willing, apparently, to blow themselves up wearing sweaters that had belonged to their dead husbands and sons, ready to die because what, really, did they have left to live for? I could not feel sympathy for their cause, and certainly not for their methods. But I did understand their desperation and their suffering. I knew how Petia and my mother would feel if I were to die here; they might feel a similar desperation, though I also knew that they would never go to the same lengths to express their anger and grief.

It was these black-veiled women, more than the men, who made me feel that we were doomed. The men had laid the plans; maybe not these men, but men somewhere, men standing behind them. The women who were guarding us with bombs strapped around their waists, who displayed an incomprehensible dedication to duty, were as trapped as we were in this situation that seemed, more and more, to have only one possible outcome.

I don't know how long we stayed like that, cowering under our seats. But the next thing we heard was laughter. We looked up. It was the terrorists, laughing at us, mocking us. The whole exercise had been a joke, designed to humiliate us, to remind us of how helpless we were, how much at their mercy we were. It was the ugliest laughter I had ever heard.

When that dreadful sound stopped, there was absolute silence. No one said a word, no one moved, no one made a sound. After a long pause, the seats began to creak as, one by one, people got up off the floor and took their places again. When I looked around, I saw that most of the male terrorists had gone, leaving the women still in their places, sitting or standing at regular intervals around us, their hands on the detonators.

A long time passed before I could think calmly again. I took a deep breath and looked around me. Some people appeared glassy-eyed and stunned. Others slumped in their seats, staring at the floor, not talking to the people beside them. There was no sense of relief in their air. It was as though we all knew that we'd just been through a dress rehearsal for death.

23

OUTSIDE THE HOUSE OF CULTURE

Thursday, October 24

The command centre, in a small building a few hundred metres from the theatre, was a hive of activity all day Thursday. Inside, Special Forces officers, deputies from the Duma, and other politicians were milling about in cramped, smoke-filled rooms, and the air rang with the constant warbling of cellphones and the crackling of two-way radios. Groups of men and women were hunched over computer screens. Parked just outside were government limousines with shaded windows. The mayor of Moscow, Yuri Luzhkov, was there, along with a handful of Chechens, the wives and relatives of political prisoners, who had been brought to the centre on the strength of promises that their loved ones would receive reduced sentences if they could persuade the terrorists to release some hostages.

One of the people at the centre was a journalist with the London *Sunday Times,* Mark Franchetti. Earlier in the day, Franchetti had talked his way onto a small delegation that included Iosif Kobzon, a popular singer who was also a member of the Duma, and two relief workers who were taking medicine into the theatre. He had been inside the theatre when the terrorists released Peter Low, the English hostage with a heart condition, and three terrified little girls and their mother. He watched as a terrorist stroked the hair of one of the girls and told her not to worry. Franchetti asked to talk to Movsar Barayev but was told that he was "resting."

Now Franchetti was back at the centre, trying to reach Movsar on his cellphone. Explaining, through an intermediary, that he had reported on the Chechen wars, Franchetti persuaded Movsar to give him an interview. Movsar asked him to bring a television camera along with him, and to come alone. After clearing it with the Kremlin—a process that took several hours—Franchetti attempted to call Movsar back to confirm that he was coming, but couldn't get through. By now it was the early hours of Friday morning.

Franchetti was let through the cordon, then walked across the desolate parking lot in front of the theatre, his progress covered by concealed snipers. It was only about forty-five metres to the entrance, but since Franchetti hadn't been able to contact Movsar, he wasn't sure the interview was still on; it was a long, tense walk. To be on the safe side, he put his hands in the air, hoping the terrorists would recognize him and not shoot.

When Franchetti reached the entrance, he saw that one of the glass doors had been shattered by gunfire. He poked his head through the opening, calling out his name as loudly as he could. When there was no reply, he waited awhile longer and then gingerly stepped into the foyer. The ground-floor lobby was a shambles, broken glass and layers of dust and plaster everywhere. There was an eerie silence: the cloakroom with its abandoned coats, hats, and scarves a poignant and disturbing reminder of the hundreds of hostages just a few metres away. Franchetti walked over to the staircase, where he was met by several gunmen, who searched him thoroughly before letting him walk up to the first floor.

Movsar's right-hand man, the one Franchetti had talked to earlier in the day during his first interview, was there to meet him. This time, however, he'd taken off his mask. The lieutenant, backed by two masked terrorists, searched him again, paying special attention to his video camera, perhaps mindful of the fate of Ahmed Shah Masoud, the Northern Alliance commander in Afghanistan who had been blown up two days before September 11, 2001, by men posing as television journalists carrying a camera packed with explosives. The three men then led Franchetti into a storeroom just off the second-floor foyer, where the staff who ran the theatre's food and drink concessions kept their wares and cashed out.

The room was cramped and small, with large refrigerators and shelves along the walls. Wallets and handbags, bottles and cigarettes were strewn on the floor. Movsar walked into the room carrying his AK-47 and a cellphone in a holster next to a grenade in his belt. He sat down and talked to Franchetti while three armed men stood behind the journalist. During the conversation, Movsar's cellphone kept ringing.

"This is a dream come true," Movsar told Franchetti. "Our spirits have never been higher. We feel great. Our task was to come here and take hostages. We have done that. Now we have no plans to leave with the hostages. We don't care. Our aim is not to stay alive. It is to force Russian troops out of Chechnya. We are not terrorists. If we were, we would have demanded millions of dollars and a plane to escape."

Franchetti saw in Movsar a vain, cocky young man who was not above feeling pride in his dubious achievement. Playing on that side of him, Franchetti was almost able to persuade Movsar to let him inside the theatre to videotape the hostages. However, Movsar's lieutenant argued strongly against it, and Movsar finally deferred to him. But he couldn't resist parading three of the women suicide bombers in front of Franchetti, explaining to him exactly what their roles were, and how the bombs they had strapped onto themselves worked. "Just let the Russians try to break in—the whole place will explode," he said.

An hour later, Movsar allowed a crew of two journalists from NTV, a privately run national network, to come inside for another interview. Dr. Roshal came too. This time there was a deal: the journalists recorded a statement by the terrorists who, in turn, said they would release twelve hostages if the statement was broadcast and showed the terrorists in a good light.

By late Thursday evening, many of the parents and relatives of those children being held as hostages had been confined to the gymnasium on Melnikova Street for almost twenty-four hours. Dependent on what they could glean from television, on what new arrivals were able to tell them, and on what their loved ones inside the theatre told them via cellphone, they were becoming increasingly angry with the authorities. They had no real news; they were frightened and tired and desperate to do something to help.

When they received word that Iosif Kobzon had met with the terrorists and would be seeing President Putin for a debriefing, they quickly drafted a letter to Putin, pleading for the lives of their children and urging him to negotiate with the terrorists. More than two hundred parents signed the letter, and they managed to get it to Kobzon before he left for the Kremlin. They were later told that the Duma had refused to accept the letter on Putin's behalf.

Toward midnight there was a flurry of calls from the hostages, passing on an urgent message from the terrorists: "Organize a demonstration! Unless you organize a demonstration against the war in Chechnya by tomorrow, they will start shooting us." Immediately the ad hoc committee got to work. Through the early morning hours, they drew up lists of friends, co-workers, members of the media—everyone they knew—and telephoned them to ask for support. When they called the mayor's office for permission to organize a demonstration, they were told they needed to get permission from the federal government. The government refused, but by this time they'd had enough of red tape: they planned to go ahead with it anyway.

24

THE HOUSE OF CULTURE

Friday, October 25   3:00 A.M.

By now, we had been held hostage for almost thirty hours. Although I was very tired, my mind was racing. I had no faith in the desperate requests I was hearing all around me, begging the Russians to do something, to negotiate, demonstrate, not to attack. There wasn't much that I could do except fantasize about escape. Over and over again, I replayed in my mind the scenario in which I would grab a pistol from one of the women. That was the easy part. The exit closest to me was now locked, but I knew which woman had the key, and even which pocket she had put it in. Could I grab the key and open the door before they shot me?

As I was thinking of this, one of the Chechen men standing in the aisle near me put down his AK-47, leaning it against the wall about two metres from where I was sitting. I felt a momentary urge to make a lunge for it. I know I could have killed a few of the terrorists. And that I probably would have been killed, too, along with other hostages the Chechens would kill in revenge. The only thing that could possibly work would be thirty or forty of us acting at the same time, each one trying to take out a terrorist. But I couldn't imagine how it could be organized, or how we could beat the odds. That is, I couldn't imagine how we could stage an uprising in a way that would actually save lives. This kind of thinking was a dead-end street, the stuff of fantasy.

I tried to remember all the hostage-taking movies I had ever seen, but I couldn't think of a single one that even remotely resembled the situation we were in. There always seems to be a good cop outside the building trying to talk the terrorists into giving up; then there's the heroic guy on the inside who is bristling with schemes for getting the other hostages out alive. There's a bomb with a digital clock so you can watch the seconds tick away before the final catastrophic explosion. The hostage-takers are usually megalomaniacs who would rather destroy the world than surrender.

The hostages, though, never have big roles in these movies. Their actual experience isn't important. It's their impending death that matters. Their presence is meant to make the movie scarier, and to make you wonder how you would behave in a situation like that. And what I wondered now was whether I could take anything from these movies to use in this situation.

I kept coming back to one point: the best hostage-taking movies have great negotiators. They talk to the terrorists or the bank robbers or the crazed father and try to get them to release some hostages to show good faith, to confide in the negotiators, to make the hostage-takers feel at ease, give them the sense that there's a way out that doesn't involve shooting or blowing up people, while getting them to give up vital information without realizing it, information that will help the rescuers devise a plan of action. Most important, though, the negotiator is the hostage-takers' only contact with the outside world, the only person they can turn to, the one person authorized to listen and talk with the terrorists.

That's what was missing here. There were so many volunteer negotiators gathered outside the theatre that there wasn't time for the hostage-takers to talk with them all. Where was the single, brilliant negotiator, the expert, the one person the terrorists had to talk to if they wanted to make any headway? I could see no evidence that such a person existed here. Meanwhile, the confused way the Russian authorities were dealing with them was only making the terrorists more and more frustrated and unpredictable and therefore more dangerous.

But even if my imaginary negotiator had been on the job, what would he or she say to terrorists who claimed that what they wanted was death for themselves and liberation for their country? Was the agony of the Chechen people something the Russians could fix in a few hours, the way—let's say—the agony of a solitary nut who was angry at the world might be temporarily assuaged? And was there any way of negotiating with terrorists who were probably awaiting orders from somewhere else? I was afraid we might never know the answers.

It was now the middle of Thursday night. Things were relatively calm. The room was quiet, except for the muffled sounds of people sobbing or praying. I could hear the murmur of quiet conversations here and there. Some people were talking to the women suicide bombers, and even, occasionally, to the male terrorists. Then I realized something. Though I couldn't hear what they were saying, I could tell from the tone that these conversations were not confrontational. People were no longer asking, "What next?" In the absence of help or direction from the outside, hostages were left to take matters into their own hands. They might not have been plotting grand escapes, but they were doing the only thing that could help now: talking to the terrorists and getting them to talk—about anything—about their lives, their hopes, their fears, religion, death. It was not something planned, or expressed out loud; it might not even have been a conscious decision. But what was really happening, I realize now, was that we were doing for ourselves what the government was apparently unwilling or unable to do. We were becoming our own negotiators.

25

CONVERSATIONS, THE HOUSE OF CULTURE

When it came to what motivated them, the Chechen women were more interesting than the men. It was not hard to imagine how men were drawn to a cause like theirs. Chechen men had been preparing themselves to fight, in one way or another, ever since they were boys. It was expected of them, just as I was expected to go to university, get a good education, and then try to make something of myself in the world. But the women were not raised to be suicide bombers. They were expected to be at home, to have lots of children, and to look after their husbands. In Chechnya, this meant taking on the whole burden of domestic life, of earning a meagre living and keeping a household going in the most appalling conditions, often with no help from their husbands, even if they were alive. Some of them were clearly well educated, but what drove them here was not anger about their plight as women. Their anger came from elsewhere.

Initially, some refused to talk, but as the hours dragged on, even the most sullen began to open up and hostages attempted to engage them in conversation. One of the hostages was a twenty-eight-year-old Russian woman who had bought a ticket to see *Nord-Ost* because her job, indeed, her life, depressed her and she wanted to escape for an evening. On Wednesday, her purse, with all her documents in it, had been stolen, and she could barely face the thought of having to replace them. Then she discovered the ticket to *Nord-Ost* in her coat pocket. She took it as a sign that she should go to see the play and forget about her troubles for a couple of hours. When the terrorists took over the theatre, it seemed like a cruel joke. Since then, she'd mostly been brooding about her life, and none of the other hostages ventured to talk to her. The Russian woman found the silence oppressive, so she kept trying to draw the suicide bomber sitting next to her into conversation. At first, the Chechen woman, who was really just a girl, ignored her, looking away whenever the Russian woman addressed her. But the Russian persisted, and eventually the Chechen spoke.

"You ask me why I'm here? I'll tell you," she said. "Last year, my brother was killed; a year and a half ago, it was my husband. I have no one left in my family. That's why I came here."

"But what you are doing is wrong," the Russian woman responded.

"Yes, I know what we are doing is wrong. But look at me—what have I got to lose?"

Georgi Vasilyev, the producer and impresario of *Nord-Ost*, was in the theatre when the terrorists attacked. He could have escaped but chose instead to remain because, as he said later, "These people"—meaning the audience—"are my guests, and I can't abandon them now."

Vasilyev had been very busy since then, communicating with the terrorists, showing them around, doing everything he could to keep tensions at a minimum. At one point, he deliberately sat next to the Chechen woman closest to the large bomb in the middle of the theatre. His aim, he said, was to engage her in conversation, thinking that if it came to the worst he could grab the detonator and disarm her. She recognized him and they fell into a conversation about *Nord-Ost*. She had seen the show, she said, and had enjoyed it. They talked about theatre and music, two subjects about which she seemed well informed. Finally, she handed him a piece of paper with Arabic words written on it. "If you repeat these words when you are about to die," she instructed him, "you will go to heaven." The words were *"la ilaha illallah"*—"There is no God but Allah."

In the balcony, a student got into conversation with one of the Chechen women about the banner they had put up. He asked her what was written on it, and was given the standard answer: "There is no other god but Allah, and Mohammed is His prophet. Freedom or death!"

"'Freedom or death' is Che Guevara's slogan," the student said. But the Chechen woman had never heard of Che Guevara.

A man sitting next to him joined in the conversation. "What do the sentiments on your banner have to do with your situation?" he asked. He wasn't challenging her; he was truly perplexed.

She said the Russians had killed her brothers.

"But then aren't you mixing up religion with personal revenge?" the young man asked.

She said nothing. So he pushed on. "Do you know anything about the history of Islam? Are you sure you're doing the right thing?"

He could see that she was trying to tune him out, so he said, "Look, wouldn't it be better if you just abandoned your explosives? What good will you do if you kill innocent people? Won't our deaths just add to the amount of evil that's already out there in the world?"

That got a response. "It doesn't matter what I want," she replied. "I have to do what I'm told to do. If I get the order, or if I see anyone from the Russian Special Forces, I am supposed to detonate the bomb. And that's what I will do."

A man sitting next to the student leaned over and whispered, "She's not going to blow anyone up. She's afraid."

One of the male terrorists who was listening to this conversation overheard him and retorted: "She's a suicide bomber—a *shakhid*—and she has come here to die." That was the end of the discussion.

More of these conversations took place. Some hostages found them encouraging because they thought they detected in the women terrorists a reluctance to take part, a hint that they might still break free from the confines of their suicidal obligations and turn the tables. It allowed the hostages to hope that if the Russian troops attacked, we might stand a chance. One woman reported that she had seen some of these young women quietly weeping: perhaps they did not have hearts of stone after all.

For others—and I would have to include myself in this group—this seemed a false hope. The women, however tragic their stories, however sympathetic they might have occasionally seemed, and however they might have regretted what they were doing, seemed clearly committed to carrying out their mission. To me, they seemed even more dangerous than the men. Their enigmatic appearance, with only their eyes and hands visible, gave them an aura of mystery. But really there was no mystery. As the hours passed and they scarcely wavered, it seemed to me that they were already dead, certainly that there was something inhuman, almost robotic, about them. I was convinced that they believed in their God, Allah; that they believed in a life after death; that they believed in the cause they were fighting for. "Not just any kind of peace," as one of them said, "but a real peace. We are tired of this war and we want it over with."

One way or another, they would get their wish.

26

RUSSIA

1999–2003

The second war in Chechnya, which began in the fall of 1999, set off a new rash of kidnapping. It wasn't regular kidnapping, the kind the Chechen guerrillas and gangs were adept at, the kind that can bring in large amounts of money, and dividends in the form of fear and intimidation and power. There were no demands for ransom, no holdouts, no spectacular nighttime raids, no shootouts. It wasn't even Chechens who were involved; it was Russians. And not the Russian army either, though you could say it was engaged in a kind of kidnapping of its own—legal kidnapping, some might call it—just to keep the ranks filled with teenaged boys to fight the campaign in the North Caucasus. But that was official; that was conscription.

No, these kidnappers were Russian women, the mothers of the young men who were waiting for their call-up papers or who were

147

already in the army and about to be sent to Chechnya or Dagestan, or who were already in Chechnya and Dagestan. They were mothers who had been driven to take desperate measures by the plight of their children, whose mental or physical well-being, whose very lives, in fact, were in grave danger.

The army to which their sons had been called was an army in disarray, its strength sapped by corruption, low morale, lack of equipment; an army that treated its own soldiers with callous indifference. It was an army that subjected its raw recruits to initiation rituals of astounding and often murderous cruelty, that sent its boys off to face the seasoned warriors in Chechnya before they had barely learned how to handle their Kalashnikovs; an army that was perpetually broke, or at least unable to meet its own payroll, in which officers routinely sold equipment, vehicles, weapons, and ammunition on the black market, thus indirectly, and sometimes even directly, arming its own enemies. It was an army in which the higher ranks could get rich, and the lower ranks could die in brutal firefights with a more determined enemy; an army that poisoned its soldiers with rations of tainted meat; an army in which the suicide rate was higher than the national average, which was in turn one of the highest in Europe. It was an army that lied about the casualties inflicted upon it, sometimes by its own men; an army that often did not even provide its soldiers with proper battlefield ID so that hundreds of bodies remained unidentified for years; an army in which, for all these reasons, the desertion rate was astronomical. It was an army in desperate need of reform, yet apparently unreformable.

As the prospect of renewed hostilities in Chechnya increased in the late summer of 1999, parents of teenaged recruits, worried sick that their sons might be sent to fight in a war from which none would return unscathed in body or soul, if he returned at all, began protesting to the authorities. The Russian government responded with reassurances that only those who volunteered for service in the Caucasus region would go. President Yeltsin even issued an edict on September 16, 1999, declaring as much—or almost as much: only volunteers with a year or more of experience, it said, would be sent to the front.

Yet even as these reassurances were being issued, young men who had barely been taught to shoot were being shipped off to war. The investigative journalist Anna Politkovskaya reported, in early October 1999, that an artillery unit based in the Nizhny Novogorod region had been sending off recruits in batches after lulling them with vodka, cigarettes, and good food. The boys would indulge in the unaccustomed generosity of their officers, then stumble into bed drunk, only to be rudely awakened in the middle of the night and hauled off to Dagestan, where military action had begun.

Many recruits who had not yet gone to the front sent letters to their families describing what was going on. Employees at the local post office were told to put these letters aside, and they were subsequently destroyed. Not a single letter from the Nizhny Novogorod unit ever reached its destination. Meanwhile, the reassurances from the government kept coming, and television news reports continued to tell the Russian public that only the most seasoned troops were being sent into action.

The parents of the young recruits were desperate. Some turned for help to an unusual unofficial organization called the Committee of Soldiers' Mothers. It was founded in 1989 to help counter the plague of hazing rituals that were, and remain, routine in the Russian army. Over the next fifteen years, the committee evolved: there were now offices all over the country, mostly in small, cramped quarters that serve as drop-in centres for desperate parents or recruits on the lam. The organization gathers statistics to counter government claims about casualty and desertion rates. As the war in Chechnya became increasingly brutal, and in the absence of any coherent, credible government response, the committee began to counsel civil disobedience. To the mothers whose sons were already in the army, already dispatched to the Chechen killing fields, its advice was unequivocal: go out and steal your boys back. Take them home. Sequester them. Better to have them whole now than disabled or dead later.

Anna Politkovskaya painted a poignant image of an army of desperate Russian mothers wandering along the wartorn roads and through the devastated villages of Dagestan and Ingushetia in October 1999, looking for their sons. Sometimes they were lucky and managed to find their sons' army unit, and perhaps even to persuade, or bribe, the commanding officers to let them take their boys out for a brief, private family visit. Then they would whisk them away, back into Russia, into hiding. Some mothers actually entered army bases illegally, climbing over fences to rescue their sons.

The sons were not always willing to leave. Soldiers, even ill-treated ones, have their pride. Politkovskaya writes of Sergei, whose mother, Nadezhda, took him home and threw away the key. "I tricked him into coming with me," his mother said. "I took away his documents. I locked him in the apartment. I argued and insisted. And I'm sure I was right."

Sometimes the "kidnappings" occurred before the boys were sent to Chechnya—but not before the damage was done. Lydia, who lived in Moscow, had to overcome her son Ivan's resistance, but she prevailed and brought him home before he was sent to war. "[He] was bullied quite unmercifully in the army and returned home not entirely in his right mind. I'm the one that's bringing him round, and healing his nerves and his mind . . . The state has done nothing to treat him. So now they want my next son? Not for anything in the world."

Part of what drives these mothers to take desperate measures is the fact that neither the Russian army nor the state offers adequate compensation for soldiers who are injured while in uniform. Parents with sons in the army face the prospect of looking after a permanently disabled child for the rest of their lives, with virtually no help from the army or the government. In 1999, the compensation package amounted to about US$10 a month. By contrast, families of victims of the Kursk nuclear submarine disaster in August 2000 were given lavish compensation.

There are no official statistics on how many mothers and fathers have been turned into "kidnappers" in this way, but the numbers compiled by mothers groups across the country help complete the picture. As of early 2003, these groups estimated that there were at least three thousand non-combatant deaths in the army each year—deaths by accident, suicide, or in shootouts. Official army statistics suggest that out of a force with 1.1 million soldiers on its roster, there are between three and four thousand desertions each year; the mothers' committees estimate the number to be ten times that high.

27

THE HOUSE OF CULTURE

Friday, October 25   9:00 A.M.

Since one of the terrorists had taken my watch, my only way of estimating the time was by the activities around me. Hostages lining up to use the orchestra pit was a sure sign of morning. As people began to stir, Yassir played a tape of Islamic songs over the theatre's speaker system, as the rest of the terrorists sang along. Yassir had a pretty good baritone voice; it filled the theatre with an eerie wail that sounded even eerier when the others joined in. It was very unpleasant. Friday had begun on an ominous note.

We learned from one of the women that at about 5:00 A.M., NTV had broadcast its interview with Movsar, but without sound. Russian television viewers saw two male hostage-takers in camouflage gear, two of them masked and one—Movsar—without a mask, sitting in the theatre's concession storeroom. They had also seen camera shots of two

152

of the women suicide bombers, only their eyes visible behind their black shawls, wearing headbands with Arabic script on them, bombs wrapped in plastic strapped around their waists, each with a pistol in one hand and a detonator in the other. But the viewers could hear nothing of what was said, nothing of Movsar's statement, nothing of the oft-repeated refrain "We want to die more than you want to live."

The women told us that the government had forbidden the station to broadcast the audio portion of the video because it violated Russian laws prohibiting "extremist propaganda." The terrorists were angered by what they considered a breach of the understanding they had with NTV. But then, what did they expect? There had already been many signs that the Russians were not about to give in to their demands; this was yet another confirmation of that stance.

Objectively, of course, the Russians were right. Giving in to the demands of terrorists only encourages more terrorism. This, however, was one time I thought the Russians could easily have made a concession. The public, indeed, the whole world, now knew what their demands were; hearing them again would neither harm the Russian government nor further the terrorists' cause. A minor concession might have bought them, and us, time.

Fully awake now, I was riding an emotional roller coaster that made it hard to think clearly: first the dismay of learning that the Russians had not allowed the terrorists' message to be broadcast. Then came the news, announced by Abu Bakar, that the foreigners would be released at 11:00 A.M., which by my estimate would be in about two hours. We also heard reports—though of course we couldn't confirm them—that six more children had been released. Were the terrorists in a conciliatory mood?

This time, Irina and I refused get our hopes up. We learned, from someone who had been able to reach his country's ambassador, that the handover was planned differently this time. Now the terrorists insisted that the ambassadors come into the theatre with proof of our citizenship. Only then would we be released. I was dismayed by the news. Apart from Irina's not having proper papers, I couldn't believe the Russian authorities would let the ambassadors enter the building: the risk would be too great. What if the terrorists decided to hold them hostage? So far, the hostage-taking was mostly a Russian-Chechen crisis. If a dozen ambassadors were held captive, it would get far messier. It would practically rule out storming the theatre. In effect, the Russians would lose the initiative.

Then things began happening so quickly that it is hard to remember what occurred when. Some pipes in the basement burst and the corridors in the lowest level of the building started filling with water. In addition, the heat had gone off and the theatre was rapidly becoming uncomfortably cold. Were the Russians who were almost certainly inside the building trying to up the ante? The women who told us about the flooded basement were amused. "The Russians are offering to send in plumbers to fix the pipes," they said, as though the whole thing were a big joke. They thought the Russians were trying to infiltrate the building under any guise, and they, the clever ones, were simply not buying it.

When the temperature in the theatre began to plummet, many hostages asked to get their coats from the cloakroom. At first the terrorists refused, but we became more and more insistent and, in the interests of keeping us calm, they gave in. "But we're not getting them for you," one of the Chechen women said. "If you want to take the risk of being shot, then go ahead."

Several hostages volunteered. While they were out in the lobby collecting the coats, we waited anxiously, listening for any reaction from the Russian troops. But there were no sounds. A few minutes later, the hostages came back laden with coats. They put them in a pile and we gathered around to sort through them. Both Irina and I managed to find our coats. It was a small thing, but I was glad to have my leather jacket. Now, no doubt, some hostages would phone out the news of this latest act of generosity on the terrorists' part. How easy, I thought, to gain respectability even while holding a gun to people's heads.

About this time, I managed to borrow a working cellphone. I called Todor, who gave me a brief report on what was going on outside. He told me that earlier in the morning, parents and other relatives of the hostages had held an unauthorized demonstration in front of the theatre. I was encouraged by the news. Maybe it would put the terrorists in a better mood.

28

OUTSIDE THE HOUSE OF CULTURE

Friday, October 25

The authorities knew that they were headed for a clash with the distraught relatives, who had become increasingly frustrated and had demanded permission to mount a full-scale demonstration against the war. When it was refused, and when they insisted on going ahead with it anyway, Deputy Prime Minister Valentina Matviyenko was dispatched to the gymnasium on Melnikova Street to talk to the relatives, cool things down, and reiterate the government's official position in the strongest possible terms. She spoke for forty minutes, though she had to use a microphone to be heard over the angry remonstrations of the crowd.

"We cannot do this," she told them. "We cannot do what the terrorists are asking us to do. We cannot let them lead us like dogs. We cannot show weakness. We cannot negotiate on their terms. This will only make the situation worse. I am also a woman and a mother. I beg you to pull yourselves together. No hysterics. You need to remain calm and think logically."

Her remarks, which were perfectly reasonable, served only to further anger the already seething crowd. The question on everyone's mind was, "Where's Putin?" They believed it was vital to have someone with the highest authority speak to the Chechen terrorists.

Early Friday morning, people—the friends, co-workers, and members of the media—whom the relatives had contacted earlier began assembling in the parking lot in front of the theatre, behind the police barriers. They were chanting slogans and carrying hastily made placards that read: "Make Peace in Chechnya!" "No to the War in Chechnya!" "Peace to the World!" By 9:00 A.M., about a hundred people had gathered. *Nord-Ost* actors who had not been in the show that Wednesday evening turned up. They sang songs. The protesters were vocal but orderly, and the police did nothing to stop them. Television cameras recorded the event, but no footage was broadcast until some time later.

The demonstration was peaceful, but the authorities at the scene were not pleased. All morning contradictory information about the state of the hostages had been coming out of the theatre. One of the hostages, a reporter, told the radio station Ekho Moskvy: "We are safe and sound. It's warm, and we have water, and there's nothing else we need in a situation like this." Other reports from inside were less soothing and spoke of a growing nervousness among both hostages and hostage-takers.

To those monitoring the situation from outside, the positive reports from the hostages had a single, simple explanation: it was the Stockholm Syndrome at work. That, at least, was the interpretation Sergei Ignatchenko, a spokesman for the FSB, the Federal Security Service, gave to the Associated Press to explain the calls for demonstrations against the war that had come from inside the theatre. Later in the day, when not much was happening outside, at least one television station broadcast a series of talking heads pontificating on the Stockholm Syndrome and speculating how deeply it had infected the behaviour of the hostages. Of course, the hostage-takers who were monitoring the coverage saw it and mockingly drew it to our attention. I was angered: how could the pundits possibly know what goes through the minds of hostages, and why? Suddenly, the idea of the Stockholm Syndrome began to seem like nothing more than a tool to manipulate public opinion.

The authorities would have looked very bad had they cracked down on the distraught relatives. Deputy Interior Minister Vladimir Vasilyev issued a statement to discourage such demonstrations from spreading: "You may regard this as a warning to the hotheads who intend to stir up passions. If anything of this kind happens, we will act toughly."

Shortly after the demonstration outside the theatre, a counter-demonstration was mounted by a group of women whose sons had been killed in Chechnya. Unlike the Committee of Soldiers' Mothers, the human rights organization that had taken a strong anti-war position since the early 1990s, these women carried bellicose anti-Chechen banners proclaiming, "No negotiations with Chechen terrorists," and other slogans that, in effect, not only supported what the government appeared to be doing but seemed, under the circumstances, to be directly provocative. Their presence angered the families of the hostages, who were eager not to do anything that might unhinge the terrorists. As the two groups of parents confronted one another, an angry exchange took place. Raisa Albina, the unofficial spokesperson for the ad hoc parents' committee, was told by one of the soldiers' mothers: "Your son is inside the theatre and he is alive. My son is dead. When your son dies, you will understand how I feel."

Why were these mothers not more sympathetic with parents who could easily become as bereaved as they were? Perhaps because most of the boys who fought for the Russian army in Chechnya were conscripts from the countryside, not the sons of sophisticated Muscovites who could afford to go to the theatre and to send their children to university, and even to keep their sons out of military service. In other words, it might have been straightforward class antagonism. Or perhaps the counter-demonstration had been set up by someone from the government: state-organized demonstrations had been a fact of life in the old Soviet Union, and it would not have been difficult to revive the tradition.

While people inside the theatre were desperately trying to keep their frayed emotions in check, those on the outside were edging dangerously close to the breaking point. This was understandable. The relatives of the hostages were in limbo. Despite receiving many calls from loved ones trapped in the theatre, they could still only guess at what was going on inside, and hope that they were correctly interpreting what they heard—they didn't know if the hostages were being allowed to say what they really thought, or if they had been ordered to sound upbeat during their phone calls. They also had no idea what the authorities were planning.

Acting through the committee, the relatives engaged the officials in fierce but futile arguments, demanding more information, calling for assurances that the authorities would put the safety of the hostages first, that they would not storm the building unless all other means to settle the stand-off had been exhausted. And there were other sources of stress as well. Some reporters from the Russian media, equipped with hidden tape recorders and cameras, had managed to sneak into the gymnasium. Without identifying themselves, they were roaming among the distraught relatives, now numbering around eight hundred—about as many as there were hostages. When some journalists offered them money for the lists of hostages they had drawn up, the angry relatives set upon them and drove them from the building.

To someone unfamiliar with Russia, this might seem like odd behaviour. Why did the relatives not welcome the reporters and take advantage of their presence to publicize their deep frustration and shame the authorities into treating them as more than just an irritation? Why, instead, did they view the press as the enemy? Partly, of course, it was because the reporters had failed to identify themselves as reporters. But it was also because, for decades, the media had been a servant of the regime, not an independent source of information. Even a decade after the collapse of the Soviet system, the Russian media was, by and large, still viewed as untrustworthy, and, with some exceptions, it probably deserved that reputation. The relatives no doubt felt that anything they said to reporters might be used against them.

They were also feeling a profound impatience with the media because of the language used in television and radio news reports: the hostage-takers were referred to as "guerrillas," "terrorists," "rebels," and even "criminals." The relatives were extremely wary of anything that appeared to insult the Chechens and might trigger retaliation. In an act of self-censorship, they had begun to refer to the hostage-takers in a neutral way, as "people from Chechnya." Even without the benefit of a crash course in political correctness, they sensed the importance of using language that seemed to treat the hostage-takers with respect.

Moreover, there were strange, and still unexplained, goings-on in the gymnasium. On one occasion, the committee became suspicious of a man who had entered the gymnasium but was vague about which of his family members was in the theatre. They turned him over to the police for interrogation. Later, sniffer dogs brought in to search the gymnasium found a large bag full of explosives. The man was arrested, and nothing more was heard of him. Was he a madman or an agent provocateur? If the government knew, it never told the relatives or the public. The incident spurred the relatives to greater vigilance: they began policing themselves, and to that end, they made identification cards for everyone in the gymnasium.

On another occasion, a man sporting some kind of official badge was found wandering around the gymnasium, buttonholing parents with a claim that he had ways of procuring more detailed information about the hostages and also about the Special Forces and the government's plan. All he needed, he said, was money to buy this information. In Russia, this is a plausible story, and several parents handed him generous sums of cash. The man vanished, never to appear again.

All the relatives could do was to continue trying to be constructive. They drew up questionnaires, trying to ascertain what special needs the hostages might have. Some were concerned about family members who suffered from a medical condition—epilepsy, or diabetes, or a heart condition, or chronic hypertension. They made lists of the names, the conditions, and the medicines needed and passed the lists to the Red Cross, which by now was making forays into the building, with the agreement of the terrorists. Svetlana, whose son was inside the theatre with friends, was concerned because he was wearing new contact lenses that might damage his eyes if left in too long. She added: "Contact lens container and fluid" to the list. Later, she found out that the Red Cross had, indeed, delivered these items to him, as requested.

29

THE HOUSE OF CULTURE

Friday, October 25   Noon

Inside the theatre, the morning dragged on. The mood of the hostages was subdued; many appeared to be sleeping, or perhaps they had simply withdrawn, resigned to whatever might happen. People devised various strategies to deal with the stress. I watched one couple sitting near me painstakingly fashion a deck of cards from scrap paper. When they were finished drawing the numbers and letters on the paper, they played cards. The man seemed very nervous; his hands shook as he played, but I could see he was trying desperately to take his wife's mind off the situation. Occasionally he would force himself to smile, as though it were the most natural thing in the world to be sitting there, playing cards.

On a borrowed cellphone, I called the Bulgarian ambassador, using the direct number Todor was able to get for me. I learned that the ambassadors had had no contact with the terrorists, that they were bowing to protocol and allowing the Russian officials to command the operation as they saw fit. The Bulgarian ambassador confirmed that he had been at the theatre on time the previous morning, which was something I hadn't known, and that he was prepared, if the Russians agreed, to enter the building with papers to prove my identity.

Though common sense told me the Russians would never agree, I felt slightly better after that conversation. Movsar passed my row, and I asked him when we were going to be released. He snapped back at me, "Nobody's discussing your release right now. Nobody cares about you."

I knew this wasn't true. The ambassadors were certainly discussing our release. But it was clear from my conversation with the Bulgarian ambassador that everything was going through the Russians, and I understood by now that the Russians had no stake in obtaining our release.

But what if I was wrong? What if it was the Chechens, not the Russians, who were balking at our release, despite their talk about how this was not our war, how they had no desire to hurt us? Then an awful thought occurred to me. Those terrorists on television who had kept their masks on must have done so because they thought they had a chance of remaining alive. But by now, because there were so many soldiers outside, there was no way they could escape with their lives. So they could have been anticipating some kind of deal, like the kind the Russians had made with the terrorists at Budennovsk. If the Russians were to say, "All right, we will start withdrawing our troops. Now give us something in return," would the Chechens release the foreign hostages but not the Russians? No, I thought—and it was a very dark thought—they would ask for safe passage back to Chechnya, and they would take us—the foreign hostages—with them as protection, as human shields, as a guarantee that the withdrawal would take place as promised. And once we got to Chechnya, what then? Would we end up like those hostages who had had their heads cut off?

The prospect of our release was causing a rift among the hostages. Earlier, when I had asked to borrow a cellphone from the Russian journalist, who still had one that worked, she refused point-blank, saying, "You are leaving and we are staying behind, so don't ask for the phone any more." The solidarity of the hostages was beginning to crumble, nerves were fraying, and the situation was deteriorating.

Early Friday afternoon, we heard that the earlier agreement to release the foreigners was off and that it was now official government policy not to recognize any distinction between the status of Russian and foreign hostages. Frankly, I wasn't surprised. In fact, I had to admit that, as hopeful as I had been, there had always been something odd about the terrorists' offer to release us. The first time I believed it because I wanted to, because I had to believe it to keep going. Today, I had believed it because there was nothing else to believe. Now I realized once again that letting us go had probably never been an option.

Meanwhile, Dr. Roshal had come back into the theatre, with members of the Red Cross, to distribute medicine. He gave some blood pressure medicine to Irina and tended to many other hostages as well. When he went back outside, he carried news of a situation that was rapidly getting worse. He talked of two cases of suspected appendicitis requiring immediate surgery, hostages with heart problems, and many women who were in need of tampons. He reported a need for antibiotics, heart medicine, eye drops, and toilet paper. He said the terrorists were refusing to release those who needed surgical attention, telling him to arrange for operations to take place in the theatre. Roshal said he was afraid that these hostages would die without medical intervention. Summing up his assessment to a journalist, he said, "The majority [of hostages] will need psychological help after this. They are under immense stress because they don't know what is going to happen. This will leave its mark."

Dr. Roshal also managed to negotiate the release of eight more children, so there was a reprise of the scene from early Thursday morning, with mothers pushing their children forward to be accepted. I could hear an anguished exchange in the balcony: a mother urging her daughter to go and the daughter refusing. Another boy, who had been bypassed by the terrorists because he was too old, was crying and pleading to be released with the other kids, and his mother was telling him to stop crying and be brave. I heard rumours that someone had offered a large sum of money to the terrorists to let his child go; it was refused.

I was by now convinced that the Chechens had chosen *Nord-Ost* deliberately because they knew it was a family show with many children in the cast, and many more in the audience. I believe it was their intention to take as many children hostage as possible, because they thought that it would give them a stronger bargaining position, and perhaps make them look good when they released some of them. It's doubtful that the Chechens released them for humanitarian reasons. Perhaps they had simply counted on the anguish of the parents and the plight of the children to move public opinion and pressure Vladimir Putin into making concessions.

At two o'clock on Friday afternoon, about one hundred people gathered just outside Red Square, on an open tract of cobblestone pavement that slopes away from the Cathedral of St. Basil's just beyond the southeastern end of the square. Most of them were friends or acquaintances of relatives of the hostages and they had gathered to demonstrate against the war in Chechnya. They would have preferred to manifest their feelings in Red Square itself. It was famous for the May Day parades, in which the Soviet Union staged massive displays of its military might, but it was also the place where tiny bands of dissidents had sometimes staged short-lived protests, gathering surreptitiously and unfurling banners before being quickly bundled off by the police and sent to Siberia. All that was now history, but Red Square in the new era remained the most symbolic place to hold protests, which was why, at the first hint of demonstrations, Putin had ordered the square closed. But the Russians are a resourceful people, and they chose a place that was close enough to be virtually in Red Square though still outside its confines.

When the demonstrators assembled, they held up banners that, like those the first protesters had carried in front of the theatre that morning, called for an end to the war in Chechnya. One of them read: "What would you do, Mr. Putin, if your daughter were inside?" Others contained messages of encouragement for the hostages. Although the demonstrators were peaceful, they were eventually dispersed by the police. Local television captured the event, but the international media was riveted on the House of Culture, where a chilling addition to the arsenal of heavy military equipment had arrived—giant bulldozers and earth-movers were now standing by, ready to go swiftly into action if the building were blown up.

30

THE HOUSE OF CULTURE

Friday, October 25   3:00 P.M.

By Friday afternoon, the hostages—some eight hundred of us—had been confined together in a single space under the threat of violent death for close to forty-eight hours. We had been given almost nothing to eat and been taken on an emotional ride that had whipped us back and forth between the extremes of despair and hope. We had scarcely been allowed to move from our seats, and most of us were in a state of utter dejection, silently praying for deliverance of some kind, praying that whatever form that deliverance took, it would be quick, and soon.

The theatre was a mess, and the garbage that had accumulated—the empty juice containers, bags, discarded programs, newspapers, items of clothing—choked the aisles and the spaces between the rows of seats. Add to that the stench of human excrement combined with the body odours of hundreds of people who hadn't had the chance to perform even the most basic acts of hygiene for two days. We could only imagine what the rest of the theatre looked like—the floors covered with broken glass, plaster dust, and spent rifle shells. I have never been to Chechnya, but I imagine that, hour by hour, this theatre was beginning to remind the terrorists more and more of home.

Then, suddenly, it seemed the women suicide bombers decided it was time to tidy up. They appeared with cardboard boxes and passed them along the rows, asking us to fill them with our garbage. They rehung the banners with the slogans written in Arabic and started clearing the detritus from the apron of the stage. They could do nothing about the state of the orchestra pit, of course, but at least something was happening, and though it made no sense, the very normality of it, the return of some kind of order to the chaos around us, made some of us feel slightly better.

When I asked one of the older women what was going on, she replied that Anna Politkovskaya was coming. I had heard, via radio reports, that the terrorists had agreed the day before to see her; she was among the few people they trusted enough to let inside the theatre. All I knew about her was that she was a journalist who wrote for one of the smaller Moscow newspapers, the *Novaya Gazeta,* one of a handful of Russian papers that have provided any coverage of the second Chechen war. Her reports were critical of both sides, but especially of the Russians.

"Why her?" I asked the woman.

"Because she is a good journalist," she replied. "And because she knows what the Russians are really like, and she is not afraid to write about what she has seen."

Before she left Los Angeles for Moscow, Anna Politkovskaya wrote a statement to be read at the award ceremony where she was to have accepted her "Courage in Journalism" citation. It concluded with an appeal to President Bush to intervene with President Putin to help bring the hostage-taking to a peaceful end.

She arrived in Moscow on Friday and after talking to the hostage-takers on her cellphone went immediately to the command centre near the theatre. Politkovskaya is a middle-aged woman with two adult children; from her pictures she looks more like a librarian than a seasoned war correspondent. Despite the extreme danger—and without the approval of the Russian government—she visited Chechnya more than forty times over the course of the most recent war to cover events there and report them as she saw them. She has received many death threats and, for a time, had to go into hiding. Now she was back in the midst of things, probably not knowing whom to trust less, the officers of the FSB—the organization now in charge of Putin's entire operation in Chechnya—or the Chechens themselves.

For about half an hour, Politkovskaya waited while the matter of her entry into the theatre was debated, and finally approved, behind closed doors. It was decided that Dr. Roshal would go in with her. Some Special Forces officers accompanied them to the edge of the parking lot, and from that point, the two of them were on their own. Cautiously, they entered the building and walked up the broad staircase at the far end of the main foyer. They encountered no one. The second-floor lobby was dark and cold. A gunman in a black stocking mask emerged from the shadows to greet them. For twenty tense minutes, they waited until someone "senior" could be found to talk to her—a odd delay, given how delighted the Chechen women, at least, had seemed at the news that she was coming. While they were waiting, Politkovskaya was questioned by different terrorists, possibly to ascertain that it was indeed her and not an impostor.

Eventually, the "senior" terrorist came out—a stocky, muscular man in a mask who bore himself, in her view, very much like a trained soldier. He led her into what was probably Yuri's storeroom, took off his mask, and introduced himself as Abu Bakar. During the conversation that followed, Abu Bakar sat with a gun on his lap, for which he later apologized: "I'm so used to it," he told her, "that I don't even feel it. I even sleep with it."

Politkovskaya asked permission to bring in food, water, juice, tampons, and blankets. Abu Bakar refused everything but the water and the juice. Then Politkovskaya's reportorial instincts took over and she asked him to explain what the terrorists wanted in political terms. From his response, she realized that he could tell her only in the most general way what their political demands were. The Chechens were, he said, "a reconnaissance-sabotage battalion" that had been specially picked for this operation. She probed their connection to the renegade president of Chechnya, Aslan Maskhadov, but Abu Bakar told her that although they were loyal to him, they were fighting on their own. From what he said, and from his demeanour, she sensed that despite a high level of frustration among the hostage-takers, they all considered the very fact that they had captured the theatre and turned the world spotlight on Chechnya a success in itself. He told her that Putin had only to promise to end the war and then make a gesture of good faith by withdrawing Russian troops from one region of Chechnya within twenty-four hours. If these two conditions were met, they would release all the hostages.

"And if not?" she asked.

"Then we will stay to fight. We will die here."

As they were talking, Abu Bakar's cellphone rang. It was, apparently, Boris Nemtsov, one of the liberal members of parliament from the Yabloko, or Apple, faction. The conversation seemed to upset Abu Bakar, and when it was over, he told Politkovskaya angrily that the Russian politicians, even the so-called liberal ones, were leading them around by the nose. Only last night, he said, the war could have been stopped and this would all be over. Now he had learned that the brutal sweeping operations, the "mopping-up" of the Chechen countryside, village by village, district by district, had been stepped up. Politkovskaya was dismayed by the news. She also realized that despite appearances, these terrorists might well have been acting on their own. "They have their own anonymous war," she wrote later, ". . . and they couldn't give a damn about [Chechen president] Maskhadov, because he doesn't share their enthusiasm." Or their frustration. "As these sentiments have grown," she concluded, "[military units like this one] have either broken up or become more radical, in effect creating a parallel, isolated war over which Maskhadov has no authority."

She asked Abu Bakar if she could meet with some hostages. At first he refused, then relented. A young hostage named Masha was brought in to meet Politkovskaya, but was so terrified she could barely speak. Abu Bakar had her taken away again. "Such a beautiful young woman," he remarked, "and we have no desire for her, because our strength must be preserved for the struggle to free the homeland."

"From his words," Politkovskaya later commented dryly, "I understood that I was supposed to be grateful to him for the fact that they hadn't raped Masha."

Anna Politkovskaya returned to the theatre later in the afternoon, laden with boxes of bottled water and juice. Since she was the only person allowed to approach the theatre, she had to make several trips; the terrorists then enlisted hostages to help carry the juice and water into the auditorium.

Sometime during the day, the terrorists decided to take away our cellphones. The Chechen women, once again, took on the housekeeping task of collecting them from us. They came around with boxes to gather up the phones, which they then emptied onto the stage. This heap of technology struck me as bizarre, sitting there almost as if it were a living thing. It was emitting intermittent beeps and warbles and snatches of popular music as the phones cried out for attention. My battery is dying, some of them said in plaintive peeps. Answer me, said others. Some of the Chechens were looking for phones that still had battery power. Some played a sick game: each time a cellphone rang, they would stir through the phones to find the one ringing, and then answer it. "No, I'm sorry," they would say. "He can't come to the phone right now." Pause. "He's a hostage." And then they would burst into laughter.

Of course, the whole thing was sadistic, certainly a cruel shock to the people who called expecting to hear the voices of their loved ones on the other end. And it was disturbing to see the terrorists behaving like children fascinated by new toys.

At about 5:00 P.M., a group of male terrorists came in. One of them, who was moving about briskly, presented a shocking spectacle: he was wearing a grey business suit and a ski mask, and was carrying a gun. He seemed cheerful. The men stood around talking to each other for a while, then disappeared. I was convinced that the man in the suit wasn't someone from the outside, that he was one of the terrorists who had merely taken off his fatigues, but his presence suggested that something was about to happen. The generally cheerful mood of the terrorists didn't help.

About thirty minutes later, the men charged back into the auditorium, very agitated. They had had no word from the Russian administration, they shouted, and they were sick and tired of it. "You have until seven o'clock. If we receive no word from the Russian authorities by then, we will start shooting you, in groups of ten."

It was a few minutes past five. The government had said nothing for two days. Why should we expect it to act now, in the next two hours?

Even worse, we had no idea whether the authorities were even aware of this latest ultimatum. Had the terrorists told them the same thing? Was there anyone out there left for them to talk to?

There had to be something we could do. The Russians were clearly not interested in helping us get out, so it made no sense to appeal to them. The terrorists were angry that negotiations were going nowhere, angry that there was insufficient coverage in the media. Communications had broken down at a fundamental level, and we had to think of a way to restore them. Some of the cellphones on the stage were still working. Irina and I talked about what might be done, and she came up with a proposal that made sense. But it would have to be me who took it to the terrorists. Irina, after all, wasn't supposed to be able to speak Russian.

31

THE HOUSE OF CULTURE

Friday, October 25 5:00 P.M.

With two hours to go before the killing was to begin, I contrived to go the front of the theatre where most of the foreign hostages were sitting and began talking to them about a last-ditch attempt to persuade the terrorists to bypass the Russian media and make a direct plea to international television networks. Irina's idea—which was admittedly grasping at straws—was that we should phone our respective embassies and ask our ambassadors to organize our release in conjunction with massive international media coverage. This way, she thought, we might be able to offer the terrorists what the Russians had so recently denied them—a chance to speak directly to the world at large in exchange for our freedom. If our release were to be simultaneously covered by CNN and BBC World—even by Al-Jazeera, for that matter—in a special coordinated broadcast highlighting the war in

Chechnya, this might give the terrorists an opportunity to bypass Russian censorship and make their case directly to a global audience. It would be a straight deal: something we wanted in exchange for something they wanted. It was a long shot, but what did we have to lose? The problem, however, was finding a phone to use. For some reason, Richard Low, the English student whose father had been released the day before, still had his cellphone. I wrote him a note, asking him to contact the British ambassador. I went back to the Russian journalist, the one who had earlier refused to lend me her phone. The terrorists had let her keep two phones, and I asked her again if I could use one of them to call the Bulgarian ambassador.

"I can't give it to you right now," she snapped. "I'm talking to the press."

I listened for a moment while she was talking, and realized that she was asking whoever was on the other end to play back to her a report she had just delivered, to make sure it sounded okay.

"But this is urgent. I've talked to Movsar, and he told me to call out on your phone." It wasn't true, but it worked. Reluctantly, she hung up and handed me the phone. I dialled the Bulgarian ambassador's number, but I couldn't get through. Was he on the phone, or out of the office? I left a message, feeling very anxious. We were racing against the clock. A few moments later, the phone rang. It was the Bulgarian ambassador calling back. I explained our plan as succinctly as I could. He agreed that it might work and said he'd try to arrange something. He said he would talk to the German ambassador as well. He tried to be encouraging. "When you get out of there," he said, "we'll have a celebration at the Bulgarian embassy."

"Thank you," I said. "I hope you're right, but I really don't feel as though I'm going to survive this."

It was the first time I had admitted that to anyone else. He mumbled something encouraging and then asked if he could speak with Movsar, but I couldn't see him anywhere.

I went back to Richard to see if he'd managed to contact the British ambassador. He'd sent a message via his cellphone, but to a regular land-line number. He was extremely rattled, so I asked him to dial the British embassy, then took the phone. I explained to the receptionist who we were and that I was calling using Richard's phone.

"Oh, how is he?" the receptionist chirped. "And how is his mother?"

"They're both fine," I said. The normality of her tone was unnerving. "But we're running out of time here, and it's really important that the foreign embassies do something to help us. The situation is getting worse by the minute, and the Russian government is not being helpful and we feel abandoned." Then I explained what we wanted.

It was risky talking on the phone, though less so now, because all the Chechen men were somewhere else. For the first day or so, a couple of them were always on the stage, watching us closely, but now, it seemed, they were hardly ever present. One of the suicide bombers had seemed sympathetic earlier in the day when we thought we were going to be let go, so I figured we had nothing to lose by letting her in on what we were doing now, and why we were phoning. She was carrying a cellphone in a sheath on her belt, and at one point, she actually lent it to us, though she was probably taking a risk in doing so.

The embassies we contacted seemed to think our plan was workable, or so they told us. All that remained now was to approach Movsar. I was on edge. This was really our last chance. It was important not to fail. When Movsar came back into the theatre, I asked the Chechen woman nearest me for permission to speak to him.

Movsar was standing at the front of the theatre, near the orchestra pit, looking distracted. "I've been told I can speak to you," I said. "I have something to propose."

He looked at me and then looked away again, as if he were totally uninterested in anything I might have to say.

I pressed on: "You may remember, I'm a Bulgarian living in Canada. I know that many countries disagree with what the Russians are doing in Chechnya."

I took a breath and waited for a reaction of some kind, an expression of interest. Nothing. I persevered. "If world public opinion goes against Chechnya, it won't do your cause any good. But if you release us—and there's lots of foreign media outside—it will show that you have no desire to kill anybody, and that you are fighting for a just cause."

I hoped the last phrase might win him over or at least pique his interest. But Movsar looked as though he'd rather be anywhere else than standing there listening to me. I had to get to the point. "We've been talking to our embassies and they can arrange to have cameras there if you let us . . ."

Movsar held up his hand, interrupting me. "No," he said flatly. "That's not an issue anymore. We're not even going to discuss it. From now on, you'll all be given exactly the same treatment as the Russians." And he turned and walked away. I went back to my place, my hopes dashed. When I told those sitting around me what had happened, some started to cry.

Aleksander, as imperturbable as ever, decided to give it one more try by talking to Yassir, who still seemed the most approachable of the terrorists. Yassir heard him out, then said: "You know, we receive our orders from outside. We can only do what we are told to do. If we are told to release you, we will release you. If we are told to shoot you, we will shoot you."

For the first time since the beginning of the siege, I felt very sorry for myself. I felt a sense of loss about everything I'd ever done in my life, every effort I had made, all those years of getting an education, my

years at university. I did it all so that I could make something of my
life, so that I could get ahead. Looking forward to the future had
always kept me going during hard times and difficult patches. Now I
was sure I was going to die, either in a ball of fire or a hail of bullets.
Everything I had done would be a colossal waste. I thought of my
family: my brother, who had been like a father to me when our father
had died; Petia, alone in Bulgaria. She must have known where I was
by now, and she would be sick with worry. Most of all, I kept thinking of my mother when she last came from Bulgaria to visit Petia and
me in Toronto. I had rented an apartment in the east end of the city,
our first home in Canada. It was in a modest high-rise, filled with
recent immigrants setting out on a new life, like us. Petia and I had
rushed around, getting furniture—just a few pieces to start with. We'd
gone shopping with my mother to buy dishes, a fold-up couch, a desk
for my computer. She was thrilled. We'd bought some flowers together,
and she had remarked on how sweet they smelled. My father had died
when I was sixteen, and she had been alone, a widow, for about twelve
years. Now we were all together in Canada. It was the happiest I had
ever seen her. I remembered how delighted she was when she first
walked through the door of our new apartment. I knew that if
something happened to me now, it would kill her.

I had started out feeling sorry for myself, but now I felt even worse
about my mother. It's strange—and perhaps some of the other
hostages felt this as well—but as I was sitting there, alone, a feeling of
calm came over me. I understood that I had accepted that I was going
to die. It wasn't something I had worked out intellectually or philo-
sophically. This acceptance had, somehow, just happened. For reasons
I can't explain, I felt prepared to die. But it wasn't a feeling of resignation. The deep regret seemed to melt away, and with that out of the
way, I felt almost heroic, even though I had done nothing remotely
heroic. It was simply that I no longer cared that I was going to die. I

only regretted how my death would affect others—my mother, my brother, my wife. Petia and I had hoped to have children in the future. That, too, would no longer be.

When I look back at this moment and try to understand how I was feeling, I realize that when people are confronted with death, especially over a long period, their emotions swing wildly from one extreme to the other. First, there is the immediate, crippling fear. Then comes the swing to a stunned, dull apprehension as we settle in to wait. Another swing, and we revel in the hope of release. Then the sudden ricochet back to despair when that didn't happen. In the last forty-eight hours there had been several such violent reversals. Some were gradual, some felt more like whiplashes, and although I tried to remain cool through them all, to think straight and logically at all times, it had been impossible. Added to that was the fact that we'd had nothing to eat but a stale sandwich or a chocolate bar or two for the last two days, very little to drink, and no exercise except climbing in and out of the stinking orchestra pit. Now the mood had swung back again, and this time, I was sure that everyone in the theatre was feeling the closeness of death, the real possibility that it would come now, sooner rather than later.

People were very quiet. Aleksander and his family were still sitting apart, as they had from the beginning. Richard and his mother were supporting each other. Natalia's son was holding her as she sobbed quietly to herself. Irina and I were hardly talking to each other; we needed to be alone with our thoughts. Irina was crying, and I tried to comfort her. I touched her face and said, "Everything is going to be all right." I didn't believe it, but what else could I say?

Most people had withdrawn into themselves. It was a time to be with your God, or with something you believed in. I sensed that everyone was thinking about things that were very personal. I wondered about the children in the balcony, and how they were coping.

And then the pendulum swung back again, and I began to feel my spirits rise. This time, it felt pretty much like anger. How could these people destroy so much? How could I just sit there and let them take away everything I had made of my life? And this "holy" desire of theirs to die, the way they flaunted their stupid slogans about wanting to die more than we wanted to live! What did they know about wanting to live? Wanting to live meant working hard, building something, giving life, not dealing in death and destruction. I certainly wanted that. I felt my energy returning, but now it was different. Using Richard's cellphone again, I sent a message to Todor: "Tell Petia I love her."

I started to take a cool look around me. Near the side door, the door that Olga had been forced through to her death, there was a fuse box that I could easily reach in an emergency. If I got the cover off and managed to throw water onto it, the fuses would blow and I would be able to douse the lights, making it easier to make an escape, or to hinder the terrorists in whatever it was they planned to do. Large bottles containing several litres of water each, those which Anna Politkovskaya had arranged to bring in, were passed around. I grabbed one and placed it as close to the fuse box as I could, just in case. The terrorists had placed a large mobile ice-cream freezer from the upper-lobby concession in front of the same side doors, probably to hinder any soldiers who might come through them during a storming. They had told us it contained a bomb, but when I stood up I could see only the sickly brown sludge of melted ice cream. Might it be possible to shelter inside it in the event of a shootout?

Then one of the Chechen women made an announcement. A Russian general, General Kazantsev, who was in charge of the Caucasus region, had telephoned the terrorists to say that he would come to the theatre at ten o'clock the next morning, but only if none of the hostages was harmed. If anyone was killed, he said, there would be no meeting. The terrorists agreed and called off their ultimatum.

The woman who told us this seemed quite heartened by the news. I could tell that she, at least, was not longing to die.

This announcement did little to ease the atmosphere of deep gloom that had settled over the theatre. Why would the Russians have decided to send in a high-ranking official, one who knew the area, one who had in fact helped lead the fight against the Chechens? No one believed it would happen. It was far more likely that the Russians were simply buying time to make their final preparations for storming the theatre.

It was an awful point to have reached. All that furious telephoning, planning, scheming, negotiating; all the efforts that people—our ambassadors, our families—were undoubtedly making outside on our behalf, and now it had all been for nothing. It felt as though everyone had lost interest in us, or at least had run out of ideas. A couple of terrorists were on the stage, still rifling through the piles of cellphones and other items that had been confiscated or voluntarily given up by the hostages. There were some knives in the pile, and at one point, one of the terrorists fished out what looked like a pistol and started playing with it. As far as I could tell, it was not a real firearm but more like a gas pellet gun. It fascinated the teenaged terrorist. He pointed it in the air and pulled the trigger. There was a loud pop, and then he started sneezing. There was a sickly sweet smell in the air that might have been tear gas—the people in the front rows began sneezing and covering their eyes. The gun must have been one of those devices some people in Moscow carry around to protect themselves from mugging, a device that fired pellets full of mace, or something that would repel would-be assailants. For a long time afterward, the smell of the gas lingered in the air. It was certainly no worse than the stench from the orchestra pit.

32

THE HOUSE OF CULTURE

Friday, October 25   Midnight

Sometime in the middle of the night we heard the furious chatter of gunfire just outside the auditorium, coming from the direction of the lobby. We tensed. People screamed. Was this the moment? Some of the hostages tried to crawl under the seats; most, however, were too exhausted to respond. We had now been held captive for about fifty hours.

A door at the back of the hall flew open and two terrorists appeared, dragging in a man wearing civilian clothes. He was about forty years old, robustly built, with a torn white shirt and closely cropped hair. Blood gushed down his face. Absurdly, he was carrying a plastic shopping bag. The terrorists frog-marched him to the front of the theatre and dragged him onto the stage, where Movsar joined them. They began punching him as Movsar fired questions at him. "What's your name?" he barked. The man mumbled something inaudible.

182

"How did you get in?" Movsar yelled.

"I just walked in. No one stopped me," he said.

"You're lying!" Movsar shouted. The men punched and kicked him some more. "What are you doing here?"

"I came looking for my son."

"Really? What's his name?"

"Roman. He's been missing for two days."

"Is that so?" Movsar said. "Let's see." He stepped to the front of the apron and addressed the auditorium: "Anyone called Roman here?" No one said anything.

"No one called Roman?" Movsar repeated. "No one up there in the balcony?" The silence was terrifying.

"Well," he said, turning back to the man, who was on his knees. "There's no one here by that name. So you must be lying."

They started kicking and beating him again, and calling him a "goat"—the Chechen insult reserved for Russian soldiers. They accused him of being an FSB agent sent in by the Special Forces to spy on them.

"I think we'll just shoot you right now, goat, right here in front of everybody," Movsar spat, unshouldering his Kalashnikov.

As exhausted and beaten down as they were, many of the hostages screamed, "No, don't do that!" and Movsar, as if deferring to them, said, "All right, then, we'll shoot him outside." And they pushed the man off the stage and up the aisle, into the upper lobby.

The whole auditorium was silent and hushed, waiting for the sound of gunfire, but none came. I'm not sure how long we sat there in the tense silence, but suddenly, I heard a scuffling noise behind me. Looking around, I saw a tall, fair-haired young man wearing glasses climbing rapidly over the backs of the seats. He was brandishing an empty juice bottle in his hand like a weapon and was heading straight for the female terrorist who was perched on the back of a seat next to the big bomb in the middle of the theatre, with the detonator in her left hand. There was pandemonium. People started screaming, calling for the man to stop, to go back to his seat. I glanced round at the stage in time to see one of the terrorists unsling his Kalashnikov, take aim, and fire off several rounds at the man, while people around him dove for the floor. There were more screams. A group of terrorists burst into the room, and Movsar yelled something in Chechen.

The shooter on the stage, as it turned out, had missed his target but the terrorists quickly grabbed the man who had tried to attack the woman and started dragging him out of the row of seats. I saw his eyes. He had the crazed, terrified look of a man who had reached the breaking point and snapped. The terrorists were shouting at him, pushing him toward the stage, beating him as they went and threatening to shoot him. Some of the hostages protested, and again, Movsar complied. They rushed the man out of the auditorium, and this time we heard gunfire.

In the turmoil immediately after the shooting, we had not seen what had really happened. The terrorist had missed the man he was shooting at, but he had hit two other people: a young man sitting close by and a woman—a young mother, as it turned out. The young man was shot in the head, and the woman was hit in the abdomen. A nurse sitting in front of us immediately got up and ran to the back to see what she could do to help. One of the women suicide bombers went with her. The rest of us were ordered not to stand up, so we had to crane our necks to see what was happening. A man was holding the woman in his arms, trying to move her toward the aisle, crying out, "Help me! They've killed my wife, they've killed her." People crowded around. The young man was sprawled back across the seats, blood pouring from his head. The husband was yelling for his daughter: "Come, oh, please come. Your mother's dying. Come, say goodbye to her." A young girl left her seat and rushed over to the man holding his wife.

The nurse came back to her seat. "There's too much blood," she told us. "There's nothing I can do. It's not first-aid these people need, it's an ambulance. They have to get to a hospital. The woman is losing so much blood she might not survive. And the boy's been shot right through the eye. He's dying."

Just then Movsar rushed back in and hurried over. He took a cursory look at the young man and, incredibly, said, "It's nothing. They can give him an eye transplant." Then, struggling to keep calm, he addressed the hostages. "People, you have to understand," he said, plaintively. "We *had* to shoot him!" At first, I wasn't sure who he was referring to—the fellow who had tried to attack the suicide bomber, or the one who had been shot through the eye. Then Movsar made the sign with his index fingers beside his forehead, meant to signify goat horns. "He was acting like a goat," he said, "and we had to shoot him. He caused a woman to be hurt, and that's against Muslim law. He had to die for it."

But Movsar wasn't finished, and we understood what was really upsetting him. It wasn't the honour of the wounded woman he was concerned about: he was afraid the Russians would think they had started executing hostages. He was afraid the incident would trigger an attack. "We have to make telephone calls. Call the Red Cross," he pleaded. "Tell them to come and pick up the injured. And when you talk to them, tell them the whole thing was an accident. Tell them we are not shooting hostages."

"But you took away our phones," someone said.

Movsar handed his phone to a woman sitting in front of us.

"What number should I call?" she said.

"Call the Moscow emergency number," he said.

The woman dialled, then waited for what seemed an excruciating length of time. Then she gave a long explanation of where we were and what we needed. She was put on hold. So she hung up and dialled again. For the next twenty minutes, no one answered the phone.

Movsar was upset. "Look how much they care!" he said. "They're not even coming to rescue you. They don't even care about the wounded."

Finally, the girl sitting in front of us said that her husband was a doctor and that he was certainly outside. "Can I call him?" she asked Movsar. "I can get him to help."

Movsar gave her the phone. When she got her husband on the other end she said, very clearly so that the terrorists could understand: "Don't worry. They haven't started shooting hostages. The whole thing was an accident. They wounded two people, but it was accidental. Please tell the Red Cross to come quickly for the wounded and then leave. This was not a deliberate shooting."

By this time, I was so exhausted I scarcely felt anything. I could only watch in amazement at what happened next. Movsar climbed onto the stage and began talking to us. It was a strange, awkward performance, as though someone not used to public speaking had to get up and persuade people to listen to him and believe him, not because of the gun in his hand but purely because of the power of his words. And words were something neither Movsar nor his fellow terrorists had ever placed much stock in.

He told us that everything was going to be fine and reminded us that General Kazantsev would arrive in the morning. "Your relatives have done what you asked them to do," he went on. "They held demonstrations calling for an end to this bloody war. What we did here now was not something we planned. We had to shoot this man because of what he did. We have made calls to the Red Cross and the emergency services. A young woman here called her husband and arranged to send in an ambulance to take them away, but they have not come. They do not care about the wounded and the dying. You must believe that we did not intend this to happen; you must understand why we had to shoot him. He might have triggered an explosion. He caused harm to others. We have no intention of taking your lives. Everything is going according to plan. Kazantsev is coming. We do not want to kill you. If the Russians do attack, I will make sure that you are protected here, behind the stage. We will not kill you, and we will not let the Russians kill you."

Movsar was upset and rambling. It was such a bizarre performance that some of the hostages started laughing, but it was a nervous laughter, the kind of thing people do when they are terrified and can't help themselves. Movsar may have been rambling, but he was also thinking of ways he could stave off an assault by the Special Forces, because the next thing he said was: "I'd like the Americans to call their embassy. Tell them the Americans have been doing a good job pressuring the Russian government and we are grateful to them for that. And to show our gratitude, we are going to let the Americans hostages go."

There were three Americans in the audience beside Sandy, though two of them were American only in the sense that they held green cards, which allowed them to work and earn money legally in the US. One of them asked what time they would be released. "Whenever you and your embassy are ready," Movsar said.

When the news was translated for Sandy Booker, he was cheered up. Sandy was sitting a few rows behind us, and Aleksander, Irina, and I decided that we should try to send a letter out with him. We indicated this to him in gestures, and he nodded agreement. Then he closed his eyes as if he were planning on having a nap before the journey to the outside. Irina borrowed a pen from Kira, Aleksander's sister, and began to write a letter to the American ambassador—an appeal, really, asking the Americans to intervene with the Russians to prevent more bloodshed.

As Irina was writing, I looked around. For some hostages, Movsar's speech had a calming effect. They seemed reassured that something positive was going to happen. They knew that supplies were running out, that even the terrorists were getting tired of waiting and, despite their efforts to keep their spirits up by singing, and shouting *"Allahu akhbar!"* at odd intervals, they were fading as much as we were. Besides, Kazantsev was a high-ranking official, so if he really were meeting with the terrorists, something decisive would happen.

The surest sign that people were feeling more optimistic was that among the hostages, some of the women started opening their hand-bags, bringing out mirrors, combing their hair, and putting on perfume and makeup. Not everyone, of course, felt that way. I certainly didn't. But it was still oddly reassuring to watch these little everyday rituals resurfacing after a harrowing two days of fear and privation. Some people began exchanging addresses, business cards, email addresses, and telephone numbers, as though a convention, or a conference, or a holiday were over and it was time to go home and resume normal life. Many people, like Sandy, were settling into their seats and allowing themselves to fall asleep, perhaps for the first time. Was I wrong about what might happen? Maybe things would turn out well, after all.

A terrible fatigue settled over me, and I closed my eyes, thinking of locks and keys and fuse boxes and ice-cream freezers. I saw myself overpowering the suicide bombers, single-handedly rescuing the entire theatre in a daring move that stunned the terrorists into inaction while the rest of the hostages got out of their seats and fled. I saw myself leading Irina to freedom over a pile of bodies on the floor.

I heard shooting in the distance, and wondered how we'd managed to get out alive. The shooting grew louder, and I could hear the terrorists crying out, not in voices of encouragement, but in panic and fear: *"Allahu akhbar! Allahu akhbar! Allahu akhbar!"* Then I remember nothing.

33

THE HOUSE OF CULTURE

Saturday, October 26   5:00 A.M.

The storming of the Dubrovka House of Culture really began many hours earlier and several kilometres to the south, in an almost identical complex called the Meridian House of Culture. Like the *Nord-Ost* theatre, it is a 1970s-era Soviet-style complex designed to house a number of activities at once, and it is laid out roughly the same way, with a twelve-hundred-seat theatre at its centre, surrounded by rehearsal halls, foyers on two levels, a large cloakroom on the ground floor, broad marble staircases on each side leading to the mezzanine, and a warren of corridors, offices, and dressing rooms, with utility rooms and the heart of a vast heating and ventilating system in the basement.

On the morning of Friday, October 26, employees at the Meridian House of Culture were given the day off with no explanation. Military vehicles pulled up to the complex and members of the Alpha Squad,

189

the elite storm troopers of the Russian Security Forces, poured out and took up positions. These highly trained operatives, skilled in the art of killing and renowned for taking no prisoners, were there for a final rehearsal before mounting a real assault to retake the House of Culture on Dubrovka Street. It was a secret operation, away from cameras and the press.

Although the Special Forces troops were prepared to storm the theatre at any moment, the decision to begin the attack had to come from general headquarters. But its control was shaky at best. On one occasion, an attack was nearly triggered by a drunken Moscow police officer who showed up in front of the theatre in camouflage gear and tried to grab a weapon from one of the soldiers, shouting: "We will kill them all!" The Special Forces detail took the rifle from him and knocked him out. When they checked his ID, they discovered that he was a general-lieutenant, one of the highest ranks in the police force. When the man came to, his first question was: "Did the Chechens shoot me?"

The main problem preoccupying FSB strategists was how to disable the terrorists quickly and completely, before they had a chance to blow up the building. By Friday, they had a top-secret plan ready to execute. It involved the use of a weapon that the Russians would probably rather not have deployed in such a public forum. They clearly now felt they had no choice. It was the very secrecy of the plan, the reluctance of the FSB to reveal the exact nature of the weapon to anyone, not even its own operatives, that would lead to tragedy for so many.

Later that night, probably while the terrorists were distracted by the arrival of the man claiming to be a distraught father, members of the Alpha Squad began smuggling the secret weapon into the theatre basement, an area they had controlled almost from the beginning of the siege. This weapon was contained in pressure tanks, and along with those tanks came two men described as "professors." Under their supervision—

at least that is how a member of the Alpha Squad later described it to the Russian media—the soldiers made openings in the ventilation system and prepared to release the contents of the tanks directly into the system, which would convey it to every corner of the complex and release it into the air. The soldiers said later that they were not told what the substance was, but that the "professors" reassured them it was "not prohibited by international conventions." This reassurance was almost certainly an afterthought, added to the official account when questions of its legality were raised in the aftermath of the rescue, mainly by the American press.

While they were in the basement, the soldiers monitoring the theatre heard the gunfire as the young man with the juice bottle lunged at the woman terrorist, and the later shots as the terrorists executed him in the lobby. They also observed some of the male terrorists changing out of their camouflage gear and into civilian clothes, as though they were getting ready, in the event of an attack, to pass themselves off as hostages and escape.

Just as Movsar Barayev had feared, the Alpha Squad analysts seemed to have indeed decided that the terrorists had started to execute hostages. But there are curious discrepancies in the timing. Some Russian accounts say the assault began shortly after the shootings. But that simply doesn't jibe with what many hostages remember. At least several hours—not fifteen minutes—elapsed between that incident and the storming, and during that time, at least one call was made from inside the theatre asking for medical assistance for the man and woman who were wounded and stressing that the shootings were an accident. (The Red Cross came and took them away.) According to Russian sources, the terrorists may even have made a direct call to the command centre asking for a medical evacuation, though they claim the Chechens did not make it clear that the shootings were spontaneous, not the deliberate initiation of plans to start murdering the hostages. Still, it is hard to believe that the Russians did not know about the other frantic calls by hostages, relaying the terrorists' message. And if they did know, then the timing of their attack was dictated not by a desire to intervene before more lives were lost but by their own strategic needs. And that makes what happened in the aftermath all the more inexcusable.

Inside the theatre, things had calmed down to the point where many hostages had finally managed to fall asleep. The terrorists seemed equally relaxed. Some of them even asked Georgi Vasilyev, the writer and producer of *Nord-Ost,* to show them the videotape of the hostage-taking captured by the theatre's security cameras. They crowded into the sound booth where Vasilyev and Sasha Fedyakin, the lighting technician, were struggling to get the video equipment working. Why were the terrorists so intent on seeing a taped version of the hostage-taking? Like Palestinian suicide bombers, Chechen fighters routinely made videotapes of their exploits for propaganda and recruiting purposes. During the hostage-taking, one of the terrorists had gone round the theatre with a small video recorder, filming the ordeal. Whatever their purpose now, their fascination with the security videos seemed to indicate they believed they were in no immediate danger of attack by the Russians. Did the Special Forces, listening in, know this? And was this the real reason why it chose that moment to unleash their secret weapon? If so, then the FSB had never had any intention of allowing Kazantsev to negotiate. That promise was, in all likelihood, a ruse.

The order to attack came around 5:00 A.M. on Saturday, October 26. We had been hostages for fifty-six hours. I remember almost nothing of what happened during that fateful fifty-seventh hour. I had been dozing when the gas started seeping through the ventilator grille nearest to where we were sitting. I vaguely remember dropping to the floor and Irina handing me a wet kerchief, urging me to breathe through it. Everything after that is a blank.

The Alpha Squad waited several minutes—fifteen by some calculations, longer by others—until they were sure the gas had taken effect. One indication that it had was that through their listening devices, they could hear loud snoring in the theatre. Just before going in, the squad members all said farewell and asked each other for forgiveness, a ritual they enact each time they go into action, in case some of them don't survive. They were equipped with flak jackets, gas masks, and assault weapons; white cloths were tied around their sleeves so they could quickly identify each other in the gloom. They had a single, overwhelming objective: to get to the terrorists before the terrorists were able to detonate the explosives.

The assault was two-pronged. The squad sequestered inside the gay nightclub located in the northeastern corner of the building blew a large hole in the wall that separated the club from the backstage area of the theatre and swarmed down on the terrorists from behind. Another force that had assembled in a hospital across Melnikova Street stormed in through the front doors, spread out across the lower lobby, and ran up the two staircases and along the corridors. They knew there were booby traps everywhere, but there was no time to disarm them. Just inside the glass doors, the soldiers ran into a volley of gunfire from a small group of terrorists, who also lobbed a grenade at them. The Russians fired back, killing the terrorists instantly, then ran up the stairs and headed for the storeroom where Movsar and his men had given the interviews. As they approached, they took fire from the room, which they returned, then tossed two grenades through the door and turned and ran down the rear entrance to the theatre, bursting into the auditorium from the back.

Another group had rushed to the left of the cloakroom on the main floor and was about to enter the corridor where Olga had been executed when a terrorist stepped out in front of them and raised his gun at almost point-blank range. The leading man in the squad was faster, killing the terrorist instantly. Without a pause, the soldiers sprinted the remaining fifteen metres to the door, past two booby traps, kicked down the double door, and were inside the theatre.

The squad that had come in from the gay club had flushed many of the terrorists forward, trapping them on the stage, where they killed them. Swiftly, like angels of death, the soldiers moved through the theatre. They now turned their attention to the women terrorists, many of whom were already unconscious, executing them on the spot. One Alpha Squad soldier saw a Chechen woman sitting on a chair as he came through the door. She was still conscious, a detonator in one hand and a pistol in the other. "Kill the bitch!" someone yelled. She managed to fire off a few rounds in the soldier's direction before she was killed by a bullet to the head. She was holding a grenade, and one of the soldiers eased it gently from her hand, then saw that she'd removed the pin. He quickly tossed it through the door, where it exploded in the hall. Hard on their heels came a special bomb demolition squad, which began the delicate work of defusing the bombs, while the Alpha troops finished mopping up, shooting on sight any remaining terrorists they could find.

It was all over in a few minutes. Incredibly, apart from a few grenades, none of the explosives had been detonated, and all but a handful of the terrorists had been killed—or "neutralized," to use the soldiers' own euphemism. It had been swift, efficient, and ruthless. When the shooting stopped and the damage could be assessed, it was discovered that some members of the Alpha Squad who had taken off their masks to improve their marksmanship had succumbed to the gas; others had suffered gunshot wounds and cuts from broken glass. But all had survived. Now those that could still walk started carrying out the hostages. There were almost eight hundred bodies in the theatre, slumped in their seats, or lying in the aisle, unconscious and breathing with difficulty. Irina and I were among them.

34

THE HOUSE OF CULTURE

Saturday, October 26 6:00 A.M.

Miraculously, some of the hostages remained conscious after the gas had been introduced. Oleg Golub, the young actor whose mother, Raisa Albina, had been keeping vigil with the relatives in the school gymnasium nearby, was still awake. Oleg had been dancing at the opening of the second act of *Nord-Ost* when the terrorists had pushed him off the stage. Someone sitting close to him during the siege had speculated that the Special Forces might use gas and advised him that if there were such an attack, he should try to breathe through his sleeve. When they smelled the gas, everyone in his row got down very low in their seats and put their noses into the crooks of their elbows. Oleg noticed that some of the terrorists had respirator masks, the kind worn by demolition workers to protect themselves from dust. One of the suicide bombers was having trouble putting hers on, and, incredibly, a hostage showed her how to do it.

Breathing through his sleeve seemed to have worked for Oleg, for though the gas made him giddy, he remained alert enough to be aware that Russian soldiers were in the building and that some were asking him about two men in his row who were unconscious. "Are they terrorists?" the soldiers asked. Oleg told them they weren't. Then the soldiers led him out through the back, through the blast hole in the wall, and into the gay club, where he waited for more hostages to be brought out before being bussed to the hospital.

Aleksander Zeltzerman remained conscious for part of the time. He remembers no shooting before the attack, and no sign that anything was happening until he saw the gas, a yellowish vapour, seeping into the theatre from the vicinity of the stage. It didn't affect him right away. Then he heard shouting, and cries of *"Allahu akhbar!"* as the terrorists realized that something was wrong. Someone yelled at Georgi Vasilyev to turn the ventilation system on; Vasilyev shouted back that it had never been turned off. The terrorists frantically opened doors to try to dilute the gas in the auditorium with fresh air, though of course there was no fresh air; the entire building, inside the auditorium and out, was filling with fumes. Aleksander saw Chechen men rush out, heading for the front of the building and leaving the women suicide bombers behind in the theatre. He heard rapid bursts of gunfire from the direction of the lobby, then an explosion. He lost consciousness for a time, and when he woke up, the commotion had died down and everyone around him seemed to have been knocked unconscious. He found himself lying back in his seat in the twelfth row, and the next thing he remembers is two men picking him up under the arms and yelling, "Run!" They frog-marched him up the aisle as fast as they could, but not before he glimpsed some of the women suicide bombers draped over the theatre seats, looking as if they were asleep.

The parking lot outside was floodlit, with crowds of people—soldiers, police, firefighters, ambulance drivers, and onlookers—milling about. There were very few ambulances as yet, but a number of city buses had pulled up outside the theatre. Aleksander couldn't see any doctors. When they reached the street, the two soldiers spun him roughly around, pushed him toward a wall, and told him to put his hands on the wall and spread his legs. As they were frisking him, he tried to explain. "It's okay," he said. "I'm a citizen of Lithuania. I've got my passport right here in my pocket."

The soldiers took his documents, along with all his money and his driver's licence, and left him standing against the wall. He never saw his documents or his money again.

Aleksander looked around and realized that he was probably one of the first people out of the theatre. Soon he was joined by a *Nord-Ost* actor, still in costume. They spoke briefly while the police searched the actor, who was very upset. "Why are they doing this to us?" he said.

"They think we're terrorists," Aleksander replied.

"Do I look like a terrorist?" the actor said.

"Maybe not, but look at me," Aleksander said. "I'm a Jew and I haven't shaved for three days. How do they know I'm not one of them? Relax, it will all work out. At least we're alive."

The Special Forces men returned. By now three hostages were pressed up against the wall. The Russians put them through a process they call "filtration," something that most Chechens know only too well. It's an effort by the police, often conducted none too delicately, to separate the innocent from the guilty. First they tied Aleksander's hands behind his back with a belt, then they took him off to a room, where he was interrogated. He asked for a glass of water, since the gas had made him very thirsty. They refused. He asked to make a call to his embassy. They refused. But they did untie his hands. Then they asked him a lot of questions, in a belligerent manner, as though he were a prime suspect. How did he come to Moscow? How long had he been here? Why was he here? What had he been doing for the past three days, and so on. Aleksander answered each question patiently, and after half an hour or so, they concluded that he was not one of the terrorists and began treating him less aggressively. Still, they continued questioning him for the next three hours. Only then did they allow Aleksander to call the Lithuanian embassy. His second phone call was to friends, who told him that his mother and sister were in a local hospital, alive and well.

Meanwhile, the comatose bodies of nearly eight hundred hostages were gradually being taken out of the theatre. If the Special Forces had been able to dispatch the terrorists quickly and efficiently enough to avoid a catastrophic explosion, what happened next was far less commendable. Although they knew that casualties might result from the storming, the authorities had not summoned a well-equipped team of medical professionals to the scene. Apart from a few paramedics, there seemed to be no doctors standing by to deal with the survivors, and it took soldiers, police, paramedics, and volunteers ninety minutes to clear the theatre. None was equipped to treat victims of the drug; no one was even told what the drug was, or what antidote to have on hand. This part of the rescue operation had a single aim: to get the bodies out of the theatre and onto the street, regardless of what state the victims were in, regardless, in fact, of whether they were alive or dead.

I have seen television footage of the bodies being brought out by the rescuers. Most were hauled out draped over shoulders, or carried sling-like by their arms and legs, with little attention paid to their specific needs. Just outside the theatre's front entrance was a pile of bodies onto which the rescuers slung more, like sacks of potatoes. Some of these people may have been dead; certainly some of them were still alive.

Astonishingly, in a city of twelve million, not enough ambulances were summoned to cope with the volume of people rendered helpless by the drug, although the authorities had known for two days approximately how many hostages were inside. Health-care workers were told only, shortly before the raid, to be prepared to handle patients suffering from drug overdoses. They were not told until later which antidotes would work, with the result that doctors spent several hours testing different antidotes before they found one that was effective. One such agent turned out to be naloxone, an antidote used in cases of heroin overdose, but that discovery came too late to save many lives. Moreover, each of the bodies was searched before being taken outside, to ensure that there were no terrorists in disguise, with explosives still strapped to their bodies. This helps to explain why so many hostages woke up to find themselves partially naked. But it doesn't explain why so many, myself included, discovered their documents and money missing.

How typical, I wonder, was a story told later by an Alpha Squad member? A group of them witnessed a Moscow police officer rifling through a purse belonging to a middle-aged woman. As he bent over her inert body, searching for valuables, she started to revive. Alarmed, he kicked her in the head, knocking her out again so he could continue his looting undisturbed. The Alpha team descended on him and beat him up, but not before discussing whether they should simply shoot him on the spot and then say he'd been caught in the crossfire.

Another woman I talked to later said she woke up in the hospital with several broken ribs. Since she was fine when the knockout drug was pumped into the building, this can only have happened after she became unconscious.

When I came to, I was sitting on a bus, my pants down around my ankles. I was trembling violently and had great difficulty breathing, or even moving. I certainly couldn't speak. I had a terrible headache. I scanned the bus for Irina, but I didn't see her. The bus was in motion, jostling back and forth, and it was full of people, some with their heads thrown back as though asleep, others slumped forward in their seats or toppled over to one side. The condensation on the windows was so thick that it was impossible to tell where we were, or where we were going. It was like coming out of an anesthetic after an operation: it took me a while to remember that my last waking thoughts had been about alerting the international community, wondering if the Russian general in charge of the Caucasus region would arrive in time, and whether he could do any better than the others had done. But where were we now? We were clearly going somewhere, but where, and why, and under whose control? Then I remembered a conversation I'd had with one of the women terrorists. What will happen, I had asked her, if Putin makes some concessions? How will you get out of here?

"We will ask for a bus back to Chechnya. The hostages will have to come with us."

Oh God, I thought, I'm on my way to Chechnya. I began looking for a way to get off the bus, but I could barely move. Then I lost consciousness again.

35

AFTERMATH

When I came to again, the bus had stopped. Though I was still trembling, I managed to wipe some of the condensation off the window and look out. We were parked outside a building that could have been a school, or an apartment building. Or it could have been a hospital. There were ghostly figures in white smocks standing around the entrance, looking at the bus. Others had boarded the bus and were helping the passengers off. Some had to be carried; I could see that they were being put on gurneys and wheeled into the building. My jeans were still down around my ankles, and I tried to reach down to pull them up, but I was still shaking violently and I couldn't manage. To make matters worse, my tongue felt swollen and painful, and I had to gasp for breath.

I must have drifted in and out of consciousness, because the next thing I knew, I was being lifted up roughly and dragged off the bus and into the building. I had the impression of a long corridor and the smell of antiseptic. I was put on a bench and left there. After a while, a nurse walked by. I tried to ask her what happened, but my tongue felt so thick and my breath so short and raspy that I could barely speak and I had to repeat myself several times.

"They used sarin," she said. Sarin—I tried to remember: wasn't that the nerve gas used by Japanese terrorists in a subway attack in Tokyo a few years ago? I attempted to ask her who "they" were, but the words didn't come out right and she lost patience and walked on. I felt nauseated and couldn't work out what was going on. I thought "they" were probably the terrorists, but beyond that, I couldn't imagine what had happened. Why was my tongue so swollen and sore? Why was it so hard to breathe? Why could I barely speak? Why were my jeans down around my ankles? Where was I? And where was Irina?

Another nurse walked by. I managed to stop her and lisp out a blurred question: "Am I going to live?"

"Of course," she said in a way that made me think she was just trying to reassure me. Several other people were beside me in the hall. Some of them, I thought, were in worse shape than I was. I was still trembling violently, but the others were vomiting up something black and treacly. I could still smell the theatre in our clothes, the sour smell of body odour, the reek of the orchestra pit. I tried again to remember what had happened, but couldn't.

Eventually, the nurse came back and gave each of us an injection, then she and two orderlies took us in an elevator to a ward, where they made us lie down on beds. I remember the beds looked as though they'd been slept in, and learned later that the ward had been quickly cleared of patients to make room for the hostages. A few minutes later, the violent trembling in my arms and legs subsided and it was easier to breathe. I reached up to touch my face, but there was no feeling in my hands, and I couldn't tell if everything was intact. I managed to get to my feet, kick off the jeans, and stumble over to a mirror. Bracing myself on the washbasin, I examined myself in the glass. I looked ghastly. I had deep, black circles under my eyes, my mouth hung open, making me look slightly idiotic, and I had three days' growth of thick, black stubble. My eyes were wide open, like a junkie's. I barely recognized myself.

Then a doctor came and told us that we must try to stay conscious, that we mustn't fall asleep. I wanted to sleep more than anything, but now I was afraid that if I did, I might never wake up. So I made a supreme effort to stay awake. As I lay there, I began to feel marginally better. But I was becoming more concerned about Irina, and I couldn't shake the feeling of fear, which was strange, because I was gradually realizing that it was all over, that I had survived. But Irina? Where was she? And what kind of shape was she in? I still knew nothing of what had happened during the storming. I knew nothing of the tragedy that had, in fact, taken place. I assumed that Irina was somewhere else in the hospital. I comforted myself with the thought that if I had survived, the odds were she had too. I waited to hear. Certainly, everything would be made clear to me. It was just a matter of time.

Although I was still confused and disoriented, my mind was gradually starting to work again. I looked around the room. I could see two other beds, each with a man lying in it, looking rough, dirty, and unshaven, like me. Three men, in suits and ties, sat on chairs close to my bed. They were watching me intently, as though they'd been assigned to make sure I didn't escape. My skin is dark, and since I hadn't washed or shaved for four days, I realized they thought I might be one of the terrorists. I looked around for my leather jacket. It was missing. I felt in the pockets of my jeans, where I had kept my wallet, passport, and other papers. They were gone too. How could I prove who I was? I explained to the men—it was obvious they were with the police—what had happened, and told them that I was a Bulgarian citizen and that I could prove it if they gave me time. I felt around in my pants pocket for the scruffy ten-ruble note I'd used to scribble down the Bulgarian ambassador's number Todor had given me. Miraculously, it was still there. I handed it to the men: "Call him, please." I said. "He knows me, and he knows I was in the theatre because I talked to him from there."

I still had on my socks, and Irina's driver's licence and bank card were still hidden in one. Indeed, I had developed a welt on my foot from the plastic rubbing against my skin. I fumbled to retrieve the cards, then explained to one of the men that they belonged to a woman who'd been with me in the theatre and asked him if he would check on her whereabouts. He took them without a word.

In what seemed like a very short time, the Bulgarian ambassador, Ilian Vassilev, a tall man of about forty with the bearing and manner of a professional politician, walked through the door to the ward. His appearance had an almost magical effect on my state of mind. He was my first connection with the world I knew, proof, in a way, that I was really alive.

Vassilev looked very tired. He shook my hand and said he'd been looking for me in all the hospitals and was glad to see me. He pulled out his cellphone, dialled a number, waited a few moments, and then said, "Mr. Nedkov? Just a moment. I have Vesselin right here." He handed me the phone.

It had all happened so quickly, I could scarcely believe it. Back in the theatre, I'd already made my peace with the thought that I would never see anyone in my family again, and now here I was, talking to my brother Nicolas. "Vessi," he said. "How are you?"

What can you say in a telephone conversation? I told him I was fine, that I was feeling weak but getting better all the time. My brother told me that he'd been doing a round-the-clock vigil in Canada and, he said jokingly, that he'd made me famous. He'd been interviewed on radio and television, and articles had appeared about me in the Canadian press. As he was speaking, I could hear my mother's voice in the background. Then she came on the phone. She was crying.

"Mom, I'm okay," I said. "I'm okay. It's all right."

"Tell me the truth, Vessi," she said. "If you're okay, why does your voice sound so strange?"

"Mom, it's just a sore throat. Otherwise there's nothing wrong with me." I hoped I was right, but I didn't want her to worry. I told her I'd thought of her often in the theatre, and that I loved her very much.

I felt a little awkward about using the ambassador's phone for such calls, so I told my mother I'd be in touch later, then pressed "End."

"I'm anxious to call my wife," I said, "but she's in Bulgaria and I don't have her number."

The ambassador phoned someone at the embassy, got the number, and dialled it for me.

When I heard Petia's voice, I couldn't stop my tears. I told her I was all right, and that I loved her. She told me, through her own tears, that my brother had phoned her and that she'd been sick with worry, and that she loved me too and was coming right away to Moscow.

My world was falling back into place. When I handed the phone to the ambassador, he said, "You had us all very scared." Then, saying that he had to talk to the doctors, he left the room. At that moment, I felt an overwhelming sense of gratitude to whatever forces of fate and fortune had intervened to save my life.

A few minutes later the ambassador came back and told me he'd arranged for me to be transferred to a different ward, to something he called a VIP room, which would have a telephone and a television. I thanked him profusely, and he said goodbye.

A few minutes later, the police officer came into the room and told me that he had found Irina. She was alive and recovering, in another hospital. It was a great relief, but it would be two days before we would talk.

When the doctor came back to check on us, I asked him if I could go to sleep now. He said yes, and within minutes, I was fast asleep.

I woke up to find one of the police officers nudging me awake. He leaned over and, gesturing at my two roommates, whispered: "Do you remember them, at least enough to be certain that they're not terrorists?" I said I couldn't honestly remember. At that point a nurse came to take me to my new room, and as I was wheeled out into the hall, I saw the police officers start to question the two men.

The VIP room was a vast improvement over the public ward. It was quieter for one thing, and I immediately began to feel more rested. I tried to learn from the nurses, the doctors, and from anyone else who came into the room, what had happened during the storming and what had become of the other hostages. At first, the information I got was scanty. I learned that not everyone had survived, and that the police suspected that some of the terrorists had got away—which explained their suspicions about me and my former roommates. They were checking other hospitals, too, to make sure none had managed to disguise himself or herself as a Russian civilian. One of the terrorists had been caught outside the theatre, in civilian clothes, when he bragged to a cameraman that he'd been talking to him a couple of days before, from inside the theatre. There were rumours going around as well, they said, that some of the women terrorists had slipped through; it would have been simple enough for them to shed their explosive belts and their shawls and escape in the ordinary street clothes they'd worn into the theatre. That helped to explain what happened to one of the hostages, a Chechen woman who had gone to see *Nord-Ost* with a Russian friend, and whose story came out later, in the papers. When the terrorists offered Chechens in the audience a chance to leave at the beginning of the siege, she'd refused to identify herself out of solidarity with her Russian friend, and she'd remained in the theatre. After the storming, the Russians had arrested her and kept her in custody for a long time before finally letting her go. In their minds, every Chechen was a suspect.

Gradually, details of the full extent of the tragedy started coming out. As my condition improved, I was able to follow developments on television. The first casualty figures were low, but still shocking; over the next few days, the death toll kept rising, perhaps as more people died in hospital, or as more relatives identified the bodies of loved ones in the city morgues. I tried to get hold of newspapers and check for names I recognized. Almost all the hostage fatalities had been, directly or indirectly, a result of the gas. Tragically, Sandy Booker did not survive, nor did his fiancée's daughter. I remembered him sleeping almost peacefully near the front of the theatre, waiting for the release that never came. He seemed a robust man, and yet the gas had killed him. But still no one knew what the gas was, not even the doctors treating us. And the authorities were silent.

As for the Chechen hostage-takers, it seemed that almost all of them had been killed by the Alpha Squad during the raid. That, at least, was the final report, though there were persistent rumours that some had managed to get away, rumours that were denied by the authorities. In a way, I felt it was a great pity, since now there would be no trial. Without a trial we would never learn, at least not in a court of law, who was behind the hostage-taking, or how all the terrorists had managed to get from Chechnya to Moscow, or who had planned and financed the raid, and whether there really was any involvement of "international terrorist centres," as Putin claimed. All those questions would remain, and in place of definite answers, we would get conspiracy theories, conjecture, accusation and counter-accusation, official affirmations and official denials, but very little in the way of solid, publicly scrutinized fact.

We were all given a battery of tests to see if we'd contracted anything while in the theatre or had any adverse after-effects from the gas. (The doctors had ruled out sarin, but they still didn't know what it was.) We were also tested for HIV, though why they thought we might have contracted HIV in the theatre, I don't know. Perhaps they thought the terrorists might have intentionally infected us.

It was an odd time. On the one hand, I felt delirious with happiness simply because I had expected to die, and here I was, alive. It was like a second birth. I remember my first shower after getting out of the theatre. Todor had sent me some soap that smelled of strawberries, and I was, finally, able to wash the physical traces of the experience off my body and out of my hair and watch them swirl down the drain. I wanted to throw away my clothes as well, but the hospital didn't provide us with any garments, so I had to hang on to them. Whenever I went near my jeans, the smell permeating the fabric took me right back inside the theatre, and made me feel sick and miserable again. And I couldn't wash the experience out of my mind.

The telephone in my room was a mixed blessing. On the one hand, it enabled me to stay in touch with my family, and incidentally, to find out more about the storming and the aftermath. But I was also getting calls from the Bulgarian and Canadian media, and giving interviews from my hospital bed. One question I was always asked was what I thought of how the Russians had handled the rescue operation. All I could say was that although I felt very sorry for those who were killed, the Special Forces had saved my life, and I didn't have a right to criticize them. Given the circumstances inside the theatre, I didn't think there was any other way they could have rescued us.

Two police officers visited me, wanting to take a statement. I answered their questions as best I could, though I kept getting interrupted by phone calls. Finally one of them grew impatient and said, "Look, Mr. Nedkov, you're busy, but so are we. I've just taken a statement from someone in the next room. How different can that be from yours? Why don't you just sign here, and we'll touch it up afterward in the office." I could tell that they were just going through the motions anyway, so I agreed. I was already thinking of writing my own, more complete, version of what had happened. If the Russian police weren't curious enough now, they would have to wait.

On the third day, Irina phoned. Through the Canadian embassy, I'd managed to get a message to her with my phone number at the hospital. She was still feeling weak, but I pressed her for details, as I was eager to find out what had happened to her since the storming. She had regained consciousness on the bus and had seen me lying on my back on the floor. She tried to crawl toward me but couldn't move. She could, however, see that I was breathing, at least, and felt somewhat reassured. When the bus arrived at the hospital, all those who were conscious were taken outside and made to wait in what looked like a daycare playground. Fifteen minutes later, another bus arrived and took them to a different hospital. She remained there for a day, with no way to contact her family, or me. So the moment she felt better, she insisted on being released. When the nurses refused, Irina took action: she snuck past the security guards, went to see the hospital's medical supervisor, and insisted on signing herself out. Irina can be very persuasive, and he finally agreed. She was calling me from home, she said, and, apart from chest pains and shortness of breath, she was feeling okay. It was a huge relief to know that she was all right.

The next day, Petia arrived from Bulgaria. It was wonderful seeing her walk through the door. For a long time, we held each other, not saying a word. I knew then that my life could begin again.

36

MOSCOW–BULGARIA–
TORONTO–MOSCOW

Epilogue

I was released from the hospital on the Wednesday following the Saturday-morning raid, a week after the whole thing had begun. Irina and I had a final conversation on the phone, but in an odd way, there was nothing more to say. We were both alive and that was enough. On Friday, Petia and I flew to Bulgaria, where I was astonished to find myself being treated like a celebrity. I was interviewed on radio and television and feted as though I were a film star. Strangers recognized me on the street. It was embarrassing to be honoured like a national hero when I had done nothing to deserve it.

Yet, I was still haunted by sensations and images that had burned themselves into my brain—the stench of the orchestra pit, the harsh sound of the Chechen language, a woman's hand twiddling the safety catch on a pistol, the sound of glass shattering, the screech of tape being unspooled, the bark of gunfire, the sight of blood, the muffled sound of people crying. These images and sensations kept passing through my mind like a video stuck on a continual loop. I couldn't get the experience out of my mind. I was also haunted by questions. How had it happened? Had the terrorists really intended to die? Would they have detonated the bombs? Why did they not do so after the raid began? Who was behind the operation? And what was the drug used in the gas, and why had so many hostages died? There were, as of yet, no answers.

The Canadian embassy in Moscow rushed through my replacement papers and sent them back to me in Bulgaria, and after a brief stay with my relatives and a thorough checkup, both physical and psychological, Petia and I returned to Canada to resume our lives and begin the painful process of trying to make sense of what had happened to me. I decided that the best way to come to terms with the experience was to embrace it, to try to understand it as fully as I could.

I started digging up press coverage, both Russian and from other parts of the world, foraging for official statements and independent reports, surfing the Internet for anything connected to the story, for interviews with hostages, police, Special Forces soldiers, relatives of those who did not survive, political analysts, observers, pundits. With Irina's help, via email, I tried to contact other hostages. This was often difficult or impossible. Many of the hostages I did reach would not talk about their experience and, in some cases, were even hostile to my approaches. But it wasn't personal. Perhaps they'd decided to employ a strategy different from my own, and were intent on putting the whole thing behind them. Or perhaps they were tired of telling that story to the media, only to see it cheapened and sensationalized.

I came to realize that the story was far more complex than even I, who had experienced it, could possibly have imagined at the time. The hostage-taking and the Special Forces storming was one incident in a far larger and more complicated story. Part of that story was what happened to Irina and me inside that theatre. Part of it was how we, and others who went through the experience, dealt with it after-ward, and how it had changed our lives. And part of it was about the war and the terrorists themselves. And to get at the heart of this broader story, I would have to return to Russia.

I did not immediately understand this. When I left Moscow after the hostage-taking, I was sure that I would never return. That part of my life was over. I had no desire to see the city again. But I soon real-ized that I could not piece this story together properly without return-ing and revisiting what had happened there and talking to others who had shared this experience with me.

And so in March 2003, I found myself, with some trepidation, en route once again to Moscow, not just to find out what happened in Act Two of *Nord-Ost,* but to find out what had happened in the next act, and, in some cases, the final act, of people's lives.

By March, something like a final tally had come in. The hostage-taking and the storming of the theatre had resulted in the deaths of over 170 people. Official reports suggest that 48 terrorists, most of them Chechen, some Arab, and including 18 women, were executed on the spot by the Special Forces. Two hostages died as a result of being shot by the terrorists: the young man who had attempted to attack one of the women, and the man who was shot in the eye. Olga Romanova, who was not a hostage, was also murdered by the terrorists, as was the man who had come in looking for his son. Some 129 hostages died as a result of the raid—most of them as a consequence of the gas the Russians released into the theatre. Some had choked to death, either inside the theatre, outside on the sidewalk, where they'd been left unattended, or on the buses on the way to the hospital. More than 650 survivors needed hospitalization, and more than a week after the storming, 67 hostages and 12 rescuers had remained in hospital in critical condition. There were even a handful of people who were still listed as missing.

The international community, and particularly the US, was intensely interested in the gas that had been used. Was it a chemical warfare agent the Russians had been keeping under wraps? Or was it something they had concocted at the last minute? The Russians remained tight-lipped about it, admitting only that the gas had been a calmative opiate, a derivative of fenatyl delivered in aerosol form. The most likely candidate, according to American medical researchers, was a substance called carfentanil, a drug used mostly in subduing large animals in zoos or in the wild. But it takes an enormous overdose of carfentanil, more than ten thousand times the effective dosage, to be lethal. There was some evidence from studies done by German doctors who examined two of the hostages shortly after the attack that an anesthetic, halothane, was also mixed in with the gas. Halothane has a therapeutic index of three, which means it takes only triple the standard dose to kill someone.

But Russians health experts claimed that the drug used, whatever it was, could not have been the cause of so many deaths. I believe that while technically they are right, so many died both because the authorities were secretive about the gas, and because they simply did not think things through. There were not enough doctors on the scene, too few ambulances, limited supplies of an antidote that might have saved lives, and above all, none of the paramedics, doctors, and nurses in attendance were ever told what the gas actually was.

All in all, the events at the performance of *Nord-Ost* in the House of Culture on October 23, 2002, took a devastating toll—on the hostages themselves, including the actors and musicians; their families and friends; the backstage and administrative staff of the theatre; the members of media who covered the story; the doctors and nurses who treated the victims; the police and Special Forces soldiers who led the storming and administered the gas; the government officials who made, or failed to make, decisions; the people of Chechnya; and, finally, the terrorist network around the world, to which, however loosely, Movsar Barayev and his gang were linked. Compared with some, my story is straightforward. I survived. Irina survived. But many of the stories are unbearably sad, mostly because of the random, indiscriminate nature of so many of the deaths.

Sandy Booker's death, of course, had been big news in the newspapers immediately after the event. He had died alongside the daughter of his Russian fiancée, Svetlana, who survived. She did not accompany Sandy's body to the US, but buried her daughter in Moscow, before returning home to Kazakhstan. Igor, the founder of the Irish dance company who had been stricken with appendicitis and treated viciously by Movsar Barayev, survived and was back working with his troupe of young dancers in the House of Culture on Dubrovka Street, where we met him, briefly, for a chat. Peter Low and his mother survived; they reunited with his father and returned to England a few days after the storming. Natalia Zhirova, the Ukrainian-Dutch woman who had been so terrified for most of the time, died. Her son survived.

For weeks after the hostage-taking, the Russian press was full of stories, some poignant, some tragic, some with happy endings. Tamara Starkova, the woman who had been accidentally shot shortly before the rescue operation began and who had been rushed from the theatre in critical condition by the Red Cross, survived. Her husband and daughter, whom she had left behind, did not.

Another story that aroused great interest was that of Irina Fadeyeva, a woman who had been sitting in the balcony with her teenaged son, Yaroslav. A few hours before the storming—a time when most of the hostages felt that the end was near—Yaroslav looked into his mother's face with particular intensity, as if trying to absorb every detail. "When we get to heaven," he asked her, "how will I recognize you?"

"Don't worry, darling," she said, "I'll find you."

When the mother regained consciousness after the storming, her son was missing. For days, she searched through the hospitals, but could not find him. Eventually, she found Yaroslav's body lying in a Moscow morgue. She was told the official cause of death was asphyxiation. Sobbing, she ran her hands over his body and discovered two unfamiliar depressions in the skin on his back. She turned him over and saw that there were two bullet holes filled with flesh-coloured wax. Her anger and grief turned to grim determination.

"I've found you," she said. "And now I will join you, as I promised."

She rushed out of the morgue and hailed a taxi, asking the driver to take her to one of the bridges over the Moskva River. She offered him her wedding ring as payment, which he accepted. When they arrived at the bridge, she bolted out of the cab and jumped over the railing into the river. But the ice was so thick it broke her fall, and she survived. She took this as a sign that she should go on living.

One out of every three musicians in the *Nord-Ost* orchestra died. The irony of it was that many more might have escaped had they simply slipped out through the basement passageways. Several had even managed to do so, but then returned because they couldn't bear the thought of leaving their friends. Others were too slow in leaving the orchestra pit because they were unwilling to leave their instruments behind and so were caught as they were packing them in their cases. Volodya Zhulyov told a colleague to go ahead. "I can't leave my cello behind. It's a gift from my mother," he said. The friend escaped; Volodya was dragged out of the orchestra pit by the terrorists. It was his twenty-third birthday. He didn't survive.

Another musician, a drummer named Timour Haziev, was subbing for a colleague that night. When he left home, he kissed his three-year-old daughter goodbye and promised to be back in time to sing her a bedtime song. Timour was a Muslim, and when he called home to inform his wife, Tanya, that they'd been taken hostage by Chechen terrorists and that all Muslims were being released, she begged him to declare his faith to the terrorists. Timour refused. "These people have nothing to do with Islam," he said. "So why should I have anything to do with them? And besides, I can't just walk out and leave my friends."

Timour did not survive. His wife, an actor, was so traumatized by his death that for a time she lost the power of speech. Gradually, through therapy, she got her voice back, but she still could not bring herself to tell her daughter what had really happened to her father. Instead, she told her that Timour had gone to live on a big star and couldn't be with them anymore. The little girl seemed satisfied with the explanation. "I saw Daddy in my dreams," she told her mother. "He is happy there and he's playing his music for us. I feel his spirit everywhere, but I want to feel his hand again."

No pattern can be found in the matter of who lived and who died. In many cases there is an element of tragic irony, for those who might have been expected to survive did not, and many of those who seemed most at risk—the elderly, the sick—lived. Among the children who died, it was the story of Kristina, fourteen, and Arsenyi, thirteen, that touched people most deeply. They were members of the children's alternative cast for the show and were in the building that night rehearsing. Kristina played Katya as a teenager in *Nord-Ost,* and Arsenyi played one of the children; off stage, they were inseparable, sharing a passion for music and a dream of careers in theatre. Like the other children and instructors involved in classes and rehearsals on the third floor of the theatre, they were herded into the balcony by the terrorists on the first night, where they sat, huddled together, holding hands and crying during those awful hours. They did not survive. On a special order from the mayor of Moscow, they were buried together in the Vagankovskoye cemetery alongside some of Russia's most famous musicians and artists. Iosif Kobzon spoke at their funeral, likening them to the star-crossed lovers Romeo and Juliet. The whole of Russia mourned them.

There were so many stories—stories of those who died so needlessly and tragically on that cold October morning. For a while, Moscow became a city of funerals and seemed to be in a state of shock. But by the time I returned, people were beginning to ask questions. A number of survivors had filed a class-action suit against the municipal government, demanding reparations for lack of protection from terrorism. They may ultimately lose the suit, but it was a brave thing to do.

There were also some happy endings. One young man had gone to the performance with the intention of proposing to his girlfriend. He had brought along an engagement ring. His girlfriend did not show up, and he decided to see the show anyway. During the hostage-taking, he sat beside a young woman who was also there on her own. Over the course of those three days, they fell in love. When he was convinced that they were going to die, he told her that he loved her and gave her the ring that he had brought with him. He asked her to marry him, and she accepted. After the storming, they were separated and he could find no trace of her. He searched for weeks. When he'd almost given up hope, a hospital administrator provided him with a clue that took him to a provincial hospital in a small town outside Moscow. There he found her, gravely ill. He helped to nurse her back to health. They married in February 2003.

The committee of relatives that was struck in the gymnasium during the siege has continued with its work. Raisa Albina's son, Oleg, had, of course, survived. Viktor's teenaged daughter, Tatiana, survived. Svetlana's twenty-year-old son survived. Natasha's husband, an actor in *Nord-Ost,* survived. We arranged to meet with them after I had been to see the show. After all, I had to see the second act.

Nord-Ost and the Link production company had been decimated. Seventeen members of the cast, including two children and eight musicians, perished, along with members of the administration and technical staff of an artistic team of three hundred. The theatre was badly damaged and much of the state-of-the-art technology, the computerized mechanisms that drove the dazzling special effects, had been vandalized or otherwise destroyed.

Two weeks after the tragedy, the producers organized a concert in memory of those who had died. It was held in a large concert hall in central Moscow and the house was full. They opened with a minute's silence in memory of the dead. The cast sang songs from *Nord-Ost* and Broadway shows. The high point of the evening was the pilots' dance, which had been so brutally interrupted a few weeks before. The audience gave the actors a standing ovation and threw flowers on the stage. Portraits of Arsenyi and Kristina were projected onto the backdrop as a young girl sang "Castle in the Clouds" from *Les Misérables*. Many tears were shed.

Dr. Roshal was brought on stage to receive thanks for his efforts to release the children. He asked forgiveness for not having succeeded in saving them all. Throughout the performance, eight empty music stands stood at the front of the orchestra, representing the eight musicians who died. Yet despite the brave face that members of the cast and crew put on that evening, the fact was that the Link production company was bankrupt and homeless.

On November 13, 2002, the surviving performers, musicians, technicians, and other personnel were told that they should expect to be laid off permanently. At that moment, many were relieved, for the prospect of walking back into the building held terrors they did not wish to unleash. Georgi Vasilyev, the producer, was himself reluctant to commit to remounting the production in such an emotionally charged environment. He knew the play would now forever be linked with the hostage-taking tragedy, and he did not wish to do anything to reinforce that connection. Then there was the nightmare of dealing with the financial cost of restoring the original production and the technology that had created it. It seemed as though *Nord-Ost* had "closed" at the beginning of the second act on October 23.

But then an extraordinary thing happened. Yuri Luzhkov, the mayor of Moscow, with backing from the federal government, proposed raising funds to re-open the theatre and remount the show. The Ministry of Labour and Social Development pledged money to compensate the employees of Link, guaranteeing that the original *Nord-Ost* company would be paid during a three-month interim period. Many private individuals, small businesses, and corporations expressed their willingness to contribute to the refurbishing of the theatre. There was a tremendous outpouring of support; Muscovites embraced the idea as a symbolic, life-affirming initiative. After some soul-searching, Vasilyev was persuaded that the show must go on, if only as a way of honouring the lives of those who had perished. And so, in a renovated theatre, with revamped technology and newly installed security devices, *Nord-Ost* was born again, on February 8, 2003.

It's difficult to imagine what that second premiere performance must have been like. Each member of the cast must have been touched with an acute sense of the past that brought new depth of feeling to the songs, to the dances, to being on that stage and looking out into the auditorium where so many people had suffered and died. It was difficult enough for me to go to the theatre a few weeks later, as a member of the audience.

In fact, I was dreading it, but I knew it was something I had to do. It was just before International Women's Day, when the streets and markets in Moscow are filled with people carrying flowers. There was much embracing and shaking of hands. The mood in the city was festive, even though the streets were still clogged with dirty snow and the sky was the colour of lead.

We arrived at the theatre mid-afternoon, early enough to meet with some of the cast before the show. It was still light and a group of boys had set up a skateboarding ramp in the parking lot in front of the building—the same open area where the Special Forces had amassed their armoured vehicles and set up their sniper points. I found myself on edge, startled by the rumble of the skateboards on the tarmac and the noisy banter of the teenaged boys. In this setting, these perfectly normal sounds were invested with malevolence. I found myself shaking. I had brought roses so that I might hand one to each of my women companions, as well as to the female members of the cast I was to meet at the theatre. The roses were trembling violently in my hand.

To get into the theatre, we had to go through a stringent security check. Burly young security guards in black suits were everywhere. The lobby areas seemed brighter, more modern. The rows of seats in the auditorium, once upholstered in red, were now done in blue, and there were minor changes in the configuration of the seating, but otherwise it was much the same as it had been the evening of October 23. I looked around at what I had thought might be my final resting place. It was all there—the apron where the masked gunman had first bounded onto the stage; the orchestra pit, swelling once more with the sounds of musicians tuning up; the sliding panels that had held the black banner; the side entrance leading to the hallway where Olga Romanova was shot; the seats in which Irina and I had sat. It was an odd sensation. There was not a trace of those terrible days in October. It was as though it had all been just a bad dream and I had woken up to find myself there again, sitting beside Irina, in a pristine theatre, waiting for the curtain to part not far from the seats I had originally purchased at the kiosk near Red Square. "You'll remember me," the old woman had said. I certainly did.

The show began, and it was just as spectacular as I had remembered it. The pilots danced at the opening of Act Two, but this time, there was no interruption. The hero, Sanya, wins his wings and flies to the Arctic. By now, the Great Patriotic War is on, and he is shot down. His gigantic plane descends and lands on the stage. In the grand finale, Katya is reunited with Sanya in the north, an old ship rears up through the ice—another amazing special effect—and the music swells to a thrilling climax. Thunderous applause.

The audience filed out, picked up their coats, made their way to their cars or to the Metro and then home. I was amazed at how objective I felt, how calm and unaffected by memories, how easy it had been to return to the scene of the crime and even to enjoy the show. I was glad I had done it.

Nord-Ost closed finally in May 2003, the victim of poor audiences and declining funds. Perhaps Vasilyev had been right: too many people could not disassociate the play from the tragic events on Dubrovka Street.

We arranged to meet with representatives of the relatives committee in the New Restaurant, a café with a relaxed Middle Eastern ambience close to the theatre. We booked the back room, a comfortable private spot with warm pink walls, padded seats and cushions with gold tassels, brass lamps lit in alcoves, and pleasant music playing in the background.

Some members of the committee whose relatives had died were reluctant to talk to us, but Raisa, Viktor, Svetlana, and Natasha joined us at the appointed hour. They were a little wary, as we were recording and filming the meeting. But as the wine flowed and they relaxed, they opened up. Eventually everyone was talking at once, vying to be heard, eager to tell his or her story. Tears were shed and passionate convictions were aired. It was clear that this committee was still very much alive.

They told us how they had found their loved ones. At first, the authorities had given out no information about the whereabouts of the survivors, but Raisa, in her typical fashion, had found out that most of the actors were at Hospital 13. She and other family members had gone to the gates of the hospital and could see nurses in the windows flapping their arms like wings to signify that the "pilots" were there. The relatives understood. Eventually, the patients came to the window and Raisa recognized her son, Oleg, still in his grey World War II costume. She described how she jumped and shouted for joy, "My son is alive! My son is alive!" Later, when Oleg was discharged from the hospital, he was very depressed, and when the reopening of *Nord-Ost* was announced, he did not want to go back to the theatre and perform in the show. Raisa accused him of being a coward and declared that if he didn't get back on that stage she would never respect him again. Oleg's response was, "I'll go back if you'll come to the opening night!" Raisa assured him that she would be there with the entire family.

Svetlana told us that her son had developed a phobia about anything Muslim, particularly women with veiled faces. So she devised some extreme therapy for him. She took him on a trip to the United Arab Emirates, where he was exposed to an entire population of veiled women. It worked.

After a couple of days, parents were allowed into the hospitals and Viktor, the man with the wallet stuffed with photographs, was shown to the ward where his daughter, Tatiana, was supposed to be. Her bed was in disorder and a blanket lay on the floor. It appeared that the occupant of that bed had died and that the body had been removed. Panic-stricken, he scoured the hospital and was eventually accompanied to the ground floor, where a row of bodies lay covered with blankets, only the shoes protruding. He wandered around, looking for

Tatiana's boots. The experience was so distressing he fainted twice. Eventually, he found her in another ward—alive. As he told this story in the New Restaurant, we all wept. Then he brought out photographs of a stunningly beautiful teenaged girl in Russian national costume, holding a sheaf of wheat and standing in front of the Russian flag. He said, proudly, that she had matured since the terrible events and was participating in family decisions.

The committee's objective now was to provide support for the bereaved, particularly for children who had lost their parents, and ongoing psychological counselling for the survivors. It had been petitioning for financial assistance from the government—to function effectively it needed space, a computer, and a budget to hire part-time support staff—but its requests remained unanswered. Now it was trying to organize a meeting between parents of victims of the hostage-taking and parents of Chechens victimized by the war. Raisa was willing to go to Chechnya to talk to people there.

Just before we parted company, Raisa told us a Russian legend. In the north of Russia was a monastery surrounded by enemy forces. Seagulls from the ocean came and repelled the enemy. She saw a parallel between the committee and the gulls: the committee was weak compared with the terrorists and the Russian government, but it was relentless, like the birds in the legend. I thought of the *Nord-Ost* poster emblazoned on the front of the theatre, the white gulls in flight, the blue sky flecked with clouds.

Our final appointment was with Memorial, the human rights organization created as a dissident group in the 1980s to recover the forgotten history of repression in the Soviet Union. The symbol of Memorial is the Solovetski Stone on Lubianka Square in Moscow, placed there in 1990 opposite the former KGB headquarters in memory of the victims of political repression. The organization conducts scrupulous research into the sins of the Soviet past and, though it is now legal and above-ground, continues to struggle for access to information concealed for so long under the totalitarian ice. It has also been fearless in documenting human rights abuses in Chechnya.

We found its offices tucked away in a narrow street in the centre of Moscow, in a dusty, three-storey building with dim corridors and tiny rooms overflowing with books and old newspapers. The entranceway and the gloomy stairway were hung with faded photographs of camps in the Gulag and men and women from a bygone era. We met with the director, Oleg Orlov, who had been a volunteer hostage at Budennovsk. He was accompanied by a Russian journalist, Andrey Miranov, a former political prisoner, who acted as Orlov's translator.

We wanted to know Memorial's view of the hostage-taking and whether it could shed light on some of the nagging questions about what exactly had occurred at the House of Culture.

Their responses were cautious. The director told us that they were investigating: "We have a specialist who is organizing a poll of all the hostages who were confined in the theatre," Orlov said. "He will do thorough research to clarify the situation and only then will we be in a position to judge to what extent the state can be accused in the deaths which occurred, to what extent it was really necessary to use force at that moment, and to what extent it was acceptable to administer gas and extricate the hostages in this manner."

Orlov spoke quietly and matter-of-factly, pausing occasionally while Miranov translated. He told us of initiatives underway to bring together Russians who had been held hostage by Chechens and Chechens who had been interned by the Russians. Many non-governmental organizations and international human rights organizations were involved in trying to bring peace to the area, and Memorial was working with various groups to provide aid and set up self-help projects.

If Orlov was meticulously unbiased in his assessment of the Moscow hostage-taking, he was adamant in his condemnation of the war. "This war affects all of Russian society," he said. "Officials have developed systematic discrimination against Chechens everywhere in Russia, not only against Chechens but against Russians in other ethnic groups. They have invented a false ethnicity. They call everyone from the region 'Caucasian.' This is absolute nonsense because there are more than one hundred ethnic groups in the Caucasus. But this stereotyping of people from the East is rampant in Russian society."

Orlov described how soldiers and police officers who served in Chechnya are brutalized and alienated from normal society. "Rank-and-file soldiers," he said, "even if they themselves have not participated in violent acts, have been witness to the abuse of others. They are psychologically damaged. When they come back, they bring their experience of brutality and violence. Even before this war, the police in Russia were never law-abiding. They were infamous. This is systematic and pandemic in Russia. Now those same people, who have had a totally free hand in Chechnya, return to our towns and villages to maintain public order. In my opinion, they need long-term and profound psychological rehabilitation."

We were meeting in the basement of the building, in a large, empty room with refectory tables and plastic chairs piled against the walls. The fluorescent lighting cast a grey pallor on the intent faces around the table.

Oleg Orlov and Andrey Miranov talked for over an hour about conspiracy theories, the connections between the Russian military and organized crime, the trade in corpses, and the infiltration of Wahhabism and Islamic terrorists in Chechnya. The work of Memorial began to feel more and more subversive and dangerous—and also vitally important.

The meeting came to an end when Orlov was called away. We stepped out into the daylight. It was a grey March day in Moscow, but the gloom outside was brighter than the dismal scenarios we'd been envisaging in that basement.

After our meeting with the committee and Memorial I began to understand more clearly that any event related to Chechnya is mired in the murky ambiguities of the war, and I felt that the truth would probably remain as elusive as an infected needle in a toxic haystack.

There were still so many unanswered questions. Even the fate of the terrorists was shrouded in mystery. Clearly, most of those in the building were shot, but other sources reported that some escaped and were arrested. No official word of their fate has ever filtered through the wall of silence. Because Russian authorities refused to release the bodies of the terrorists, they were never returned to their families in Chechnya.

I had learned a great deal about the circumstances that led to this event, but I had really learned little about how it occurred—about who was really responsible and why. I had learned a great deal about myself, though, about what I valued and about how I wished to lead my life. In an odd way, the experience had been like a crash course in how to find one's way in the world. It was not the kind of course in which one would want to enrol voluntarily, but having been forced to endure it, I had survived and learned some lessons from it.

I have certainly never thought of myself as courageous or daring in any way, but I like to think I am level-headed and fairly well adjusted psychologically. I might be described as having a typically male response to emotional situations. I did not shed a tear during the final frames of the Hollywood blockbuster *Titanic,* and I believe that I have good problem-solving skills and a rational turn of mind. But few experiences in modern life ever really challenge one's self-perception or test all those fondly held assumptions about strength of character. I found

I was not immune to fear or despair, that I was not in control of my emotions when I witnessed people being beaten, abused, and executed in cold blood. I discovered that while I was consumed with a violent rage against the people who had done this dreadful thing to me, I was also able to keep at bay irresponsible devils goading me to rash decisions and impulsive irrational acts. But throughout the ordeal, I believe my salvation was a habit of logical, strategic thinking that kept me constantly occupied in trying to work out what exactly was happening at any given moment and what I should best do to prevent my own death, and the deaths of those around me.

Each human being in that theatre discovered that his or her essential personality—whatever inner resources could be mustered, whatever strength of character and moral courage had been acquired in his or her life—was on the line. We had to battle fear and panic, and struggle to keep our faith and hope. We had to learn to think clearly and think fast, and not give up. We had to rise above physical discomfort, hunger, pain, and sickness. It was a struggle against a stark and paralyzing fear of death, but when we were strong in our resolve, overcoming this fear brought out the best in us. Everyone reacted differently, of course, with varying degrees of courage and despair and panic and determination, but without a doubt, this personal struggle was the common experience of every man, woman, and child. It was a process of discovering our true selves, and we cannot now escape this knowledge of who we really are. For those of us who survived, this is a lens through which we must forever view the world. But more than that, our perspective on the world was abruptly altered. Our horizons were shifted, our awareness was heightened, our ideas were challenged.

I am not a very religious person, though I have no objection to people who are. I am a logical person. I like things to make sense. I live a comfortable life but I am not rich. I vote and express my opinions, but I'm not all that interested in politics. What's good for business usually suits me fine. I contribute in other ways to society, but I'm not exactly what you would call an activist. I am a free man. Free to enjoy life. Free to choose. Free to dream. I am Vesselin Nedkov, Bulgarian Canadian, healthy, hard working, and, until recently, oblivious to the true state of the world. There must be millions of people like me, minding their own business, watching all kinds of earth-shattering events from a distance on television, happily removed from ground zeros around the globe, untouched by atrocities and horror, unaware of the danger lurking just beneath the surface of everyday life—of our own complacency.

The terrorists interrupted the play and changed the plot of *Nord-Ost,* but they also interrupted my comfortable assumptions and changed my way of thinking. This unimaginable intrusion pitted my values against another set of values so different that my logical mind could barely comprehend them. It did not make sense to me at the time, and it still does not. My life experience, which is average and middle class, was thrust into direct confrontation with people whose experience of life was so extreme and so alien that it was hard to believe we inhabit the same planet, though Chechnya is as close to Bulgaria as it is to Moscow.

But it was not just the terrorists who jolted me out of a sense of complacency. If the terrorists brought the Chechen war to Moscow, the Russian Special Forces brought some of the tactics of its Chechen war to the theatre on Dubrovka Street. Yes, well over six hundred lives were saved, and yes, I am grateful that mine was one of them. But I will never forget how the Russian hostages feared rescue by their own soldiers almost more than they feared the terrorists. The rescue operation was conducted with ruthless and brutal efficiency, with borderline respect for the lives of the victims, but only because they were in the spotlight of the world's attention. The real heroes on the Russian side were, for me, the doctors like Shkolnikova and

Roshal, and the hundreds of hostages who managed to keep their heads under the constant threat of a horrible death.

At first, I wanted to tell this story because of its sheer drama: lots of tension and a shootout at the end. Perhaps I needed to vent my anger against the perpetrators of the crime and the senseless tragedy that followed. Perhaps I needed to justify my own survival. Perhaps, because I am an entrepreneur at heart, I saw this as a way to turn my ill luck at having been there to my advantage, a sort of survivor's dividend.

Yet in the final analysis, I am surprised to find that the most urgent reason for telling this story is quite different. The unfolding of the drama, the development of the characters, the intricacies of the plot, the dreadful denouement, the lucky escapes, the astonishing resilience of so many of the survivors and their families and the dreadful weeping of the bereaved—these elements are secondary to a central truth about what occurred in Moscow. In that theatre, every one of us became, whether we wanted to or not, a representative of values and traditions worth living for.

I remember that at the very worst moment, when I thought we were all going to die, I understood that it would be important, if I survived, to try to live well, to always treat people with respect and tolerance, not just in preparation for the final accounting when my time or luck ran out, and not just for the sake of my own family and circle of friends, but for the sake of all people, even for those not yet born. I understood that every act of violence, brutality, and cruelty, every injustice and every atrocity diminishes and threatens us all, wherever we may be. This is what I learned.

NOTES

The story in this book draws on a variety of sources, ranging from a long series of direct interviews—about fifty hours in all—with my co-author, Vesselin Nedkov, and with Irina Filipova, to interviews with other participants, eyewitness accounts found in newspapers and internet websites, and newspaper and journal stories by reporters, observers, and historians. I also travelled to Moscow with my wife and assistant, Patricia Grant, and with Vesselin and Irina, we paid several extended visits to the scene of the crime.

In a sense, all the incidents in this book, including the main action inside the theatre, are reconstructions, though each is of a different kind. The story of what happened inside the theatre is based primarily on Vesselin Nedkov's memories of the event, but we have cross-referenced them with Irina's recollections and with accounts from other participants, as well as with available timelines, those blow-by-blow accounts sometimes referred to by wire services as "tic-tocs." The confusion of the events themselves and the inevitable failings of human memory, especially under stress, mean that not everything happened exactly in the sequence presented in the book, though we have made every effort to make that sequence as accurate as possible.

In the chapters not based on Vesselin's recollections, I have drawn on a variety of sources, with the occasional injection of imagination, but always based on probability. For instance, after the hostage-taking, some of the Chechen women suicide bombers were found to have bus tickets for Moscow in their pockets purchased in Khasavyurt, Dagestan. The highly speculative journey described in Chapter 2 was based on helpful input from Russian friends and a virtual tour through many Russian sites and road maps. Likewise, the account in Chapter 19 of a woman's search for the body of her husband is based on accounts that I believe to be accurate, both from Memorial and from Russian journalists who have covered the war on the ground.

Information about the Link production company and the creation of the play *Nord-Ost* was taken from Vesselin's interviews with members of the ensemble, in particular with the artistic director, Georgi Vasilyev, and from its website, available in English at www.nordost.ru.

The history of Chechnya in Chapter 5 draws on a number of sources, the principal ones being three excellent books on the subject and the region: *Chechnya: Tombstone of Russian Power,* by Anatol Lieven; *Chechnya: Calamity in the Caucasus,* by Carlotta Gall and Thomas de Waal; and *Highlanders: A Journey to the Caucasus in Quest of Memory,* by Yo'av Karny. The information gleaned from these books was supplemented by facts and anecdotes taken from various websites, most of which are listed below, and from reports on the subject by human rights groups such as Memorial.

The chapter on the hostage-taking at Budennovsk draws on some of the above-mentioned sources, but in particular on newspaper accounts and on an article by Major Raymond C. Finch III entitled "A Face of Future Battle: Chechen Fighter Shamil Basayev," in *Foreign Military Studies Publications,* which can be found online at www.fas.org.

The reconstruction of the scene outside the theatre after the hostage-taking (Chapter 12) comes largely from daily newspaper accounts, both in the Russian and the American and international press, and from eyewitness accounts of relatives of the hostages. In describing visits inside the theatre and conversations with the terrorists by the *Sunday*

Times reporter Mark Franchetti (Chapter 23) and by the Russian reporter Anna Politkovskaya (Chapter 30), I drew mostly on their own published accounts of the events. Also of great help was the documentary *Terror in Moscow*, produced earlier this year by Mark Franchetti and Dan Reed and distributed by Mentorn Films. That documentary contains footage from a variety of sources, including a video taken inside the House of Culture by the terrorists themselves.

The account of the storming of the theatre by the Russian Special Forces is based largely on several interviews with the soldiers, published in the Russian press, and on the recollections of hostages who remained conscious during the attack. The accuracy of those accounts could not be verified independently, and they should not be taken as the last word on what happened.

Regarding the gas that was used in the storming of the theatre, we depended mainly on research published by *The Journal of the American College of Emergency Medicine*. Articles can be found at www.elsevierhealth.com. But in the absence of official confirmation from the Russian authorities, this information, like much of the background to this story, remains—as of October 2003—informed speculation.

Vesselin and I make no claims that our book is a definitive account of the Moscow theatre hostage-taking. There are still too many unanswered and, within the limits of this project, unanswerable questions. The profound impasse between the Russians and the Chechens remains unresolved, despite the recent elections in Chechnya, and is very likely unresolvable in the foreseeable future. We hope we are wrong about that, but we fear we are not. What remains is a story of innocent people caught in a vortex of violence and death. In that sense, it is the story of every terrorist act of hostage-taking.

Paul Wilson
Toronto, October 2003

SOURCES

Listed below are the secondary sources we used in writing the book. Pride of place belongs to Johnson's Russia List, at www.cdi.org/johnson. A twice-daily email from this independent source helps keep its thousands of subscribers abreast of events and trends in and around Russia. It is the best single source of up-to-date information, and it is all archived, making it a prime research tool.

OTHER INTERNET SOURCES (ENGLISH LANGUAGE):

American Foreign Policy: www.afpc.org
BBC: www.bbc.co.uk
Centre for Defense Information, *Russia Weekly:* www.cdi.org
The Christian Science Monitor: www.csmonitor.com
CNN: www.cnn.com
Federal News Service, Moscow: www.fednews.ru
Guardian Unlimited: www.guardian.co.uk
The Independent: www.independent.co.uk
Institute for Democracy in Eastern Europe: www.idee.org
Institute for the Study of Conflict, Ideology and Policy: www.bu.eduiscip
Institute for War and Peace Reporting:
    www.iwpr.net/caucasus=indexl.html
The Jamestown Foundation—Chechnya Weekly:
    www.jamestown.org/pub_chechnya
Janes Intelligence Digest: www.janes.com
The Los Angeles Times: www.latimes.com
The Moscow Times: www.the moscowtimes.com
The Muslim News: www.muslimnews.co.uk
New Times Moscow: www.newtimes.ru
The New York Review of Books: www.nybooks.com

The New York Times: www.nytimes.com
Open Democracy: www.opendemocracy.net
PBS: www.pbs.org/wideangle
Pravda: www.english.pravda.ru
Radio Free Europe: www.rferl.org
Radio Netherlands: www.rnw/nl/hotspots
Russian Democratic Party (YABLOKO): www.eng.yabloko.ru
Time magazine: www.time.com
The Times: www.times-archive.co.uk/news
The Washington Post: www.washingtonpost.com
The Washington Times: www.washtimes.com
Yahoo Chechnya Short-list:
   http://groups.yahoo.com/group/chechnya=sl

More information about Chechnya and Chechen society and culture can be found at the Chechen Republic Online, www.anima.com, which also provides a bibliography of helpful books and articles, and at www.chechnyafree.ru/english.

The Israeli-based International Policy Institute for Counter-terrorism is a good source of information about terrorism, suicide bombings, and the role of women in terrorist activities. It can be found at www.ict.org.

Information about the work of Memorial can be found at www.memo.ru. Amnesty International provides information about human rights violations in Chechnya, which can be accessed at www.amnesty.org, as does Human Rights Watch, at www.hrw.org.

Interesting material on and by Anna Politkovskaya can be found at the International Women's Media Foundation, www.iwmf.org, and at the Danish Support Committee for Chechnya, www.tjetjenien.dk/chechnya.

RUSSIAN-LANGUAGE INTERNET SOURCES USED:

Compromat.ru: www.compromat.ru
Gazeta.ru: www.gazeta.ru
Intrefax News Agency: www.interfax.ru
Izvestia.ru: www.izvestia.ru
Kommersant newspaper: www.kommersant.ru
Komsomolskaya Pradva: www.kp.ru
Lenta.ru: www.lenta.ru
Moscow News newspaper: www.mn.ru
Newsru.com: www.newsru.com
NTV Television Archives: www.ntv.ru
Novaya Gazeta: www.novayagazeta.ru
ORT Television Archives: www.1tv.ru
Polit.ru: www.polit.ru
RBK News Agency: www.rbk.ru
Regnum.ru: www.regnum.ru
REN TV: www.ren-tv.ru
Utro.ru: www.utro.ru
Vesti.ru: www.vesti.ru

One of the hostages, Aleksander Stal, has published an account, in Russian, of his experiences at http://knyajich.narod.ru/no/NO.htm.

BOOKS CONSULTED:

The following books provided invaluable analysis and background on terrorism, Russia, Chechnya, and the Chechen wars:

Dunlop, John. *Russia Confronts Chechnya.* Cambridge and New York: Cambridge University Press, 1998.

Gall, Carlotta and Thomas de Waal. *Chechnya: Calamity in the Caucasus.* New York: New York University Press, 1998.

Harmon, Christopher C. *Terrorism Today.* London: Frank Cass, 2000.

Human Rights Watch. *"Welcome to Hell": Arbitrary Detention, Torture and Extortion in Chechnya.* New York: Human Rights Watch, 2000.

Karny, Yo'av. *Highlanders: A Journey to the Caucasus in Quest of Memory.* New York: Farrar, Straus and Giroux, 2000.

Lieven, Anatol. *Chechnya: Tombstone of Russian Power.* New Haven, Conn.: Yale University Press, 1998.

Politkovskaya, Anna. *A Dirty War: A Russian Reporter in Chechnya,* Introduction by Thomas de Waal. Translated by John Crowfoot. London: The Harvill Press, 1999.

Satter, David. *Darkness at Dawn: The Rise of the Russian Criminal State.* New Haven, Conn.: Yale University Press, 2003.

Solzhenitsyn, Aleksandr I. *The Gulag Archipelago: 1918–1956.* Vol. 3. New York: Harper and Row, 1976.

ACKNOWLEDGMENTS

I would like to thank my family for being with me, supporting me through these months of emotional recovery. It was extremely hard for me to relive the horrible event that took place in Moscow and to work on this book; their love and care gave me the emotional strength to do it. Those fifty-seven hours when I was in the theatre, held hostage, were even harder for them—waiting, hoping, and praying, helpless to do anything. I know that if I had the choice of going through another hostage-taking or having to stand by while something like that happened to a loved one, I would choose the former.

This book would not have been possible without the help of Irina Filipova, who provided us with ideas, energy, and information. I will always remember her quiet courage and resourcefulness when we were faced with death. Her unique perspective on the event is part of what informs this book.

I am very grateful to my friend Todor Mikhailov, who spent fifty-seven sleepless hours outside the House of Culture. He was my lifeline with the outside world and with my family, and without his support, the enormous emotional pressure I felt inside would have been far more difficult to bear.

I would like to thank the Bulgarian authorities from the Ministry of Foreign Affairs, and particularly the minister of Foreign Affairs,

238

Solomon Passy, the Bulgarian ambassador to Russia, Ilian Vassilev, and the Bulgarian consul, Aleksander Itov, for their efforts to do everything in their power to help me through the hostage-taking and afterward, during my recovery in hospital. These are men Bulgaria can be proud of.

I would also like to thank the Canadian authorities, and especially those at the Canadian embassy in Moscow, for all their help and assistance. They showed remarkable understanding of my circumstances and were invaluable in keeping my relatives informed.

My thanks also to my friend Kiril Vasilev, who created the schematic diagram of the theatre.

Finally, I would like to thank my co-author, Paul Wilson, for helping me present my story in a way that I hope you, the reader, will find compelling.

Vesselin Nedkov
Montreal, October 2003

W hen I was first approached by Penguin to collaborate with Vesselin Nedkov on this book, I demurred. Although I had written a lot about Eastern Europe—especially Czechoslovakia—under totalitarianism and afterward, and indeed, had personal experience of the heavy hand of Soviet rule during the ten years I lived in Czechoslovakia, I knew little at first hand about Russia, and even less about its history since 1991. Given the complex political background to the war in Chechnya and the controversies surrounding the Moscow hostage-taking, I felt that my credentials were somewhat thin. When I met Vesselin, however, I was won over by his clarity about what had happened to him, by his enthusiasm for telling his story, and by his determination to tell it in a way that would be both compelling and informative to readers. His judgment was, I thought, completely right, and since he was to be the narrator, and his experience the main subject, I agreed to do it. Helping other people tell their stories is something I do know how to do as a translator and editor.

We began taping Vesselin's story of the hostage-taking early this year, when the details were still fresh in his mind. Vesselin also did an enormous amount of research through Russian sources, seeking out newspaper and website accounts of the hostage-taking, and translating the best of them for me into English. He also took on the major burden of organizing our trip to Moscow in March.

In Moscow, we met Irina Filipova, who was with Vesselin in the theatre. Her recollections and observations of the event provided an invaluable dimension to Vesselin's story. She also made arrangements for us to meet people in the *Nord-Ost* company, and on the parents committee. Later, she was our main contact person in Moscow, providing valuable secondary material and checking on facts and sources when we needed it. Most of all, though, Irina Filipova brought her own rich sensibility and her uniquely Muscovite perspective to the telling of this story. It would have been difficult to write this book without her unqualified cooperation.

I have been helped by conversations with people, in Moscow, and later in Canada, who filled in details. Some of them wish to remain off the record. Anatol Lieven and Thomas de Waal are both experienced journalists and historians who have written much about the subject of Chechnya and the Caucasus. Conversations with them—and, of course, their books—were invaluable to us in putting the events in Moscow in the proper perspective. Independent filmmakers Katerina Cizek and Peter Lynch went with us to Moscow to record the most visible part of the making of this book. Katerina was especially helpful in our negotiations with the people behind *Nord-Ost*, who were initially reluctant to talk about the tragic events that had so recently decimated their ranks.

I'd like to thank Diane Turbide, editorial director of Penguin Group (Canada), who approached me with this idea, and guided the book, with help from production editor Sandra Tooze and copy editor Judy Phillips, through its breakneck schedule. My thanks also to Barbara Epstein, of the *New York Review of Books*, who provided me with invaluable contacts in Moscow, to Larry Krotz, a Toronto freelance writer, who kindly read the next to last draft and gave me some invaluable pointers, and to Paul Webster and Jennifer Clibbon for bringing their knowledge of Russia to a reading of the final draft. None of these people, it goes without saying, are responsible for any errors that may occur in the book.

The writing of *57 Hours* coincided with another major project in my life, the start-up of a new magazine called *The Walrus*. The staff, led by editor David Berlin and publisher Ken Alexander, were kind enough to tolerate my frequent absences during the magazine's crucial start-up phase, which coincided with the final stages of writing this book. For that they have my thanks.

Most of all, though, my deepest gratitude and love go to my wife, Patricia Grant. She transcribed most of the tapes, did much of the research, and brought her considerable writing skills to bear on the book at every stage. With her background in the professional theatre, Patricia is a consummate storyteller with a keen sense of drama, and her talents were essential in helping me craft Vesselin's story. She also endured two weeks in Moscow in early March, an experience not to be taken lightly, and cracked the whip when we were falling behind in a very tight schedule. As with so much else in my life, so it is with this book: I could never have done it without her support, encouragement, and love.

Paul Wilson
Toronto, October 2003

INDEX